N·E·T·S·C·A·P·E NAVIGATOR™

QUICK TOUR

FOR WINDOWS

SECOND EDITION

N·E·T·S·C·A·P·E
NAVIGATOR™
QUICK TOUR
FOR WINDOWS

SECOND EDITION

ACCESSING & NAVIGATING THE INTERNET'S WORLD WIDE WEB

Gayle Kidder & Stuart Harris

VENTANA

Netscape Navigator Quick Tour for Windows: Accessing & Navigating the Internet's World Wide Web, Second Edition
Copyright © 1995 by Gayle Kidder and Stuart Harris

Library of Congress Cataloging-in-Publication Data
Kidder, Gayle.
    Netscape Navigator quick tour for Windows : accessing & navigating the Internet's world wide web / Gayle Kidder & Stuart Harris. --2nd ed.
       p. cm.
    First ed. by Stuart Harris.
    Includes index.
    ISBN 1-56604-371-9
    1. Netscape. 2. World Wide Web (Information retrieval system) 3. Internet (Computer network) I. Harris, Stuart (Stuart H.)
  II. Harris, Stuart (Stuart H.). Netscape quick tour for Windows. III. Title.
  TK5105.882.K53 1996
  025.04--dc20   95-50053
                                    CIP

Book design: Marcia Webb
Cover illustration: Charles Overbeck

Acquisitions Editor: Patty Williams
Art Director: Marcia Webb
Assistant Editor: JJ Hohn
Design staff: Charles Overbeck, Jennifer Rowe, Dawne Sherman
Developmental Editor: Tim C. Mattson
Editorial staff: Amy Moyers, Beth Snowberger, Melanie Stepp
Managing Editor: Pam Richardson
Print Department: Dan Koeller
Production Manager: John Cotterman
Production staff: Patrick Berry
Project Editor: Lois Principe

Index service: Dianne Bertsch, Answers Plus
Proofreader: Beth Snowberger
Technical review: Brian Little, The Imagination Workshop

Second Edition 9 8 7 6 5 4 3 2 1
Printed in the United States of America

Ventana Communications Group, Inc.
P.O. Box 13964
Research Triangle Park, NC 27709-3964
919/544-9404
FAX 919/544-9472

Trademarks

Trademarked names appear throughout this book. Rather than list the names and entities that own the trademarks or insert a trademark symbol with each mention of the trademarked name, the publisher states that it is using the names only for editorial purposes and to the benefit of the trademark owner with no intention of infringing upon that trademark.

About the Authors

Gayle Kidder is a journalist and editor with twenty years experience in books, magazines, newspapers, and documentary television. She has published over 500 articles in magazines and newspapers on topics as diverse as science, theatre, art, travel, fiction, and computers. She currently maintains an online column of cultural events for the city of San Diego at **http://w3.thegroup.net/~zoom**.

Stuart Harris is the author of *The irc Survival Guide* (Addison-Wesley) and numerous articles about the Internet in national magazines. He works as an Internet consultant and is leader of his local computer society's Internet special-interest group. He has also been involved in technical editing and TV documentary production. Stuart enjoys communicating complex ideas to a mass audience.

In addition to previous versions of this book for both Windows and Mac, they are the coauthors of *HTML Publishing With Internet Assistant* and *HTML Publishing for Netscape*, both published by Ventana. Other joint projects have included TV documentary production, journalism, software product management and, recently, a type of live theater on the Internet. Gayle and Stuart work in the classic "electronic cottage" near the beach in San Diego and are on the Net every day of their lives.

Acknowledgments

We consider ourselves lucky to have had a number of bright and capable Net wizards who cheerfully helped us in the preparation of this book.

Foremost among them is Mark Burgess of the Data Transfer Group in San Diego, a prince among Webmasters, for his unfailing generosity and expert guidance (and for giving us our first copy of Netscape Navigator).

Mike Bowen at CERFnet also provided invaluable assistance on several topics. Phil Hom at Primus Inc. was indispensable in preparing the Macintosh version of the book, for both his Mac expertise and his excellent work in providing the Mac graphics.

Brent Halliburton of Group Cortex, and Steve Sanders of the CyberSpace DataBase BBS, contributed undocumented features. Thanks also go to Gareth Branwyn for giving us, in his forerunning Ventana books about Mosaic, a good model to follow.

Most of all, we'd like to acknowledge each other. Neither of us thinks there's the slightest chance we could have turned this book out on schedule without the other's help and support.

CONTENTS

MENUS, BUTTONS & BARS 33

MAIL & NEWS 65

5 BOOKMARKS & PREFERENCES 91

INTRODUCTION

The recent explosion of interest in the Internet for personal use amounts to a headlong rush toward a new global culture. As more and more people discover the ease and speed of e-mail and the vast wellspring of information to be tapped at the touch of a key or the click of a mouse, it is as if a virtual city were being built out of thin air—overnight.

Nothing has made the resources of the Internet more accessible to ordinary people all over the world than that part of the Internet known as the World Wide Web. Born only seven years ago, in 1989, as the by-product of a European physics lab in Switzerland, the World Wide Web now links together hundreds of thousands of documents all over the world, including not just scientific but educational, business, commercial, and recreational interests as well.

Always in the forefront as the capability of the Web advances is Netscape Navigator, a software package that allows you not only to browse the Web with ease but to take advantage of all the other Internet resources with one easy interface. Netscape Navigator was the first commercial offshoot of Mosaic, the U.S. Government-developed product. Netscape used the talents of many of the bright young programmers who developed Mosaic, and it offers the same easy visual format, allowing the user to quickly search through documents and skip lightly from one to another in pursuit of items of personal interest.

In writing this guide to Netscape Navigator 2.0, which cannot help but be a guide to the Web as well, we are thinking of our typical reader as reasonably well educated but not necessarily technically inclined. Our target reader may be a teacher or a business person who wants to tap into the resources on the Web but has little time to spend learning a complex software program—the sort of person Netscape Navigator was designed for, actually. He or she may well need help getting Navigator set up—a task comparable in difficulty to programming a modern VCR (which often sends parents to their kids for help). But our prototype reader is above all someone who is ready to explore the Web with us and have some fun while picking up valuable information.

The first time you set off to explore the World Wide Web is something like entering a magic hall of mirrors. Every time you turn a corner or open a new door, another world opens up for you. One moment you may be in Boston, the next you're in Santa Cruz. Then at the touch of a mouse you're off to Tokyo, Stockholm, London, Hong Kong.

This is the amazing metauniverse that the World Wide Web has created in just a few short years. And every day, as more and more people discover the Web and begin to imagine its possibilities, it becomes even richer. In fact, the Internet has been so democratized by the advent of the Web that a student in Arkansas can now create his or her own "page" on the Web that has standing equal to that of the Smithsonian Institution or the White House visitors' page.

We assume that you already have at least an elementary understanding of the Internet, although that may not extend much beyond e-mail. Readers who feel a need for more background on the Internet are advised to pick up one of the many great books on the market now, such as Michael Fraase's *Windows Internet Tour Guide* (published by Ventana), or *The Whole Internet Book* or *Big Dummy's Guide to the Internet*. Once you've got Netscape Navigator installed, you'll be able to find excerpts from the latter two of these titles on the Web.

Hardware & Software Requirements

Before we start, there are also some basic hardware and software requirements to be met. "Uh oh," we hear you saying, "Here it comes—another upgrade." Not necessarily. Naturally, as with most powerful programs these days, the bigger your hard drive and the more RAM you have, the smoother things will be for you.

But if you've got the basics, there's no reason to run out and buy more until you explore the Web and see what kind of information you're likely to want to access. It's perfectly possible to run Netscape Navigator with a minimal configuration as long as you're not in a hurry or you're willing to do without the graphic images much of the time. Here's what you need, with an eye both on what's absolutely necessary and what's recommended to make things smoother:

- Good: 386 SX with 4MB RAM. Better: 486 or Pentium processor with 8MB RAM or more.

- Microsoft Windows 95, Windows NT, Windows 3.1, or Windows for Workgroups 3.11 in 386 Enhanced mode.

- Good: VGA monitor. Better: SVGA monitor.

- Good: 8-bit color video card. Better: 16-bit color video card.

- Good enough: 9,600 baud modem. Far better: 14,400 or 28,800 baud modem.

- A Winsock TCP/IP stack (SLIP/PPP communications software—we'll tell you how to get this later).

In addition, you should make sure you have about 20MB of free hard drive space. Netscape Navigator will need it for creating temporary directories.

And last—but most important—you will need your Internet connection. You can get this through:

- A direct connection through your institution or business.

- A private Internet service provider (more details on this in Chapter 2, "Getting Started").

- Some online services: America Online, CompuServe, and the Microsoft Network currently support Netscape Navigator. Prodigy has plans to. Check with your online service if you're in doubt.

Super-Duper Quick Start

Netscape Navigator is easy to set up and begin using on your own, providing you have a working familiarity with communications software. If your Internet connection is already up and running, and you have a copy of Navigator on disk, you can go ahead and install it yourself from the disk. Then click on the Netscape logo and you're off! Netscape will take you to its own Welcome page and from there you can follow links to whatever interests you.

Take a look around and enjoy yourself. Soon enough you'll want to know more about some of its special features. Jump ahead to Chapter 4 to learn how to use the mail and news features and Chapter 5 to use the bookmarks menu. In Chapter 6, you'll find information on using Netscape Navigator for audio, video, and multimedia applications, as well as special applications like FTP and Telnet. And since you're a quick learner, we know you'll want to figure out how to make your own Web page. You can follow our easy instructions in Chapter 7.

What's Inside

Chapter 1, "The Net & the Web," provides a brief look at the development of the Web as the newest and fastest-growing segment of the Internet. It explains how the idea of hypermedia in an easy-to-use graphical interface transformed a system once used primarily by the techno-elite into a new democratic forum.

Chapter 2, "Getting Started," tells you how to get yourself connected and set up Netscape Navigator to work on your system. In case you don't have a copy of the program on disk, or want to go get an upgrade, this chapter also gives explicit instructions on downloading via FTP. Once you're up and running, we'll take a quick cruise on the Web to demonstrate Navigator's main features.

Chapter 3, "Menus, Buttons & Bars," gives a detailed tour of Netscape Navigator's menu items and its easy-to-use buttons, so you'll know what every item on your screen does. You'll learn how to navigate the Web smoothly, and save and print interesting material you find.

Chapter 4, "Mail & News," describes Netscape Navigator's new mail and newsreading functions. You'll learn how to send, receive, and organize your e-mail in Navigator, and set up your address book for easy communications. In the News section, we'll tell you how to subscribe to any of the thousands of interesting newsgroups available on Usenet and how to get started participating in news discussion groups.

Chapter 5, "Bookmarks & Preferences," gives a guided tour of Netscape Navigator's bookmark menu, so you can keep track of all your favorite sites and organize them into neat categories for easy access. Then we'll take a second look at those Preferences that allow you to customize Navigator to suit your own taste and to set it up to work with other applications you may have.

Chapter 6, "Launching Into Cyberspace," begins by looking closely at hypermedia on the Web, explaining what you need to play audio files and view videos and animations with Netscape Navigator. Then we'll talk about using Navigator to do other things available to you on the Internet like FTP, Archie and Gopher searches, and Telnet.

Chapter 7, "Making Your Own Web Documents," is a brief primer on designing a Web page. We'll show you visually how we created a simple home page, with easy steps you can follow in designing your own Web document.

Chapter 8, "Searching & Sites," explains how to use the Web to search for topics that interest you. Then we'll look at the different kinds of Web documents available for all interests, including online publications, educational resources, museums and art galleries, business sites, travel and recreation, and some prize-winning Web sites to get you started on your own explorations.

The appendices include a guide to some undocumented Netscape Navigator features and a summary of the *Netscape Navigator Quick Tour for Windows Online Companion*, where you can find more resources to help you enjoy the Web. There's also a glossary and an index for your reference.

Nothing Stays the Same

When we got our first copy of Netscape Navigator—a Version 0.9 beta release—we were immediately impressed with its superior features, its speed, and its friendly interface to dozens of applications. During the first writing of this book, Netscape Navigator went through three subsequent beta versions to the official Version 1.0 release. Only a few months later we found ourselves revising it yet again for the Version 1.1, and now less than a year later, Version 2.0, upon which this edition is based.

We've seen a lot of changes in the way images are handled, some wonderful improvements like the addition of tables and colors and font control, impressive changes in newsgroup and e-mail handling, to mention just a few. The most exciting area of development in Netscape Navigator 2.0 is its multimedia capabilities, something we're sure is bound to develop immensely in coming months, no doubt leading to yet more revisions. But we feel confident that you will continue to find this a helpful guide to all the main features of Netscape Navigator for some time to come, and that all you learn here will be easily translatable to later versions of the software.

The future of the Web is another matter. It is changing so rapidly day by day that it's hard to say where it will all lead six months, a year, or two years from now. What is certain is that once you start looking at the Web with Netscape Navigator, you'll be as much a part of its future as physicists in Geneva, businessmen in Tokyo, and high-school students in Tuscaloosa.

Gayle Kidder
Stuart Harris
San Diego, California

THE NET & THE WEB

The world of personal computing these days is a lot like the Red Queen's kingdom in *Through the Looking Glass*—everyone seems to be running faster and faster to stay in the same place. Relatively new computer users can be forgiven for fearing that they'll never catch up.

If you've gotten as far as buying this book and acquiring Netscape Navigator however, cheer up. You can congratulate yourself for being on the leading edge of the fastest-growing segment of the Internet— the World Wide Web. As you begin to explore the Web with Netscape Navigator, the number of resources you'll find there may make you think this has been going on for a long time. How could you have missed out for so long? Relax, it's not so. Almost everything you see now on the Web didn't exist five years ago.

The Web itself was created in 1989, but it didn't become widely accessible to those outside the scientific and academic communities until the creation of the Mosaic graphical interface in 1993. It was that event that suddenly made the Web easily available and attractive to hundreds of thousands of computer users around the world. The following set of statistics gives you the idea: In June 1993 there were 130 server sites on the Web; by November 1994, approximately a year and a half later, there were more than 10,000. Current estimates place the number of users plugging into the Web at nearly five million, but the actual numbers are almost impossible to track, since, like a child's game of tag, no one ever stays still long enough to count.

Given the rapidly growing interest in the World Wide Web for educational and commercial uses, it's entirely possible that this is your first experience with "that thing" everyone's been talking about for the last few years: the Internet. And you may be just a little confused about how the Web relates to the Internet. If so, read on. By the end of this chapter, you should have a fairly clear idea of the world you're entering with Netscape Navigator. By the end of this book, we hope you'll be running alongside the rest of us in the world of computing, trying to keep up with the changes that are hitting us faster every day.

The Internet: How Does It Work?

Basically, the Internet is the architecture upon which everything else you've heard about hangs. It is nothing more (and nothing less) than thousands of computers all over the world that communicate with each other minute-by-minute over an unbelievably complicated network of cables, fiber-optic filaments, and satellite links.

Although it started—back in the Info Stone Age of the '60s—as a creation of the U.S. Government, it's important to realize that the Internet as it exists today belongs to no one country, government, or business, no matter how large or powerful, nor is it operated by any single authority.

It works something like this: Imagine that you live at the northwest corner of an unbelievably complex network of canals. You need to send a message to somebody at the southeast corner. There may be 1,000 different routes your message could take on its way from one corner to the other, and you have no way of knowing which might be the best—which canals are congested right now, which have been taken out of service for maintenance, which have been blocked by a bus or a large animal falling in. Nevertheless, you can put your message in a bottle, label the bottle "SE" and just toss it into the nearest canal. You can walk away confident that your message will get through as long as there's an agreement between the people who live on this canal system.

The agreement is this: At every canal junction there's a person who knows which routes are blocked in the immediate neighborhood. This person picks up each bottle that comes by, looks at its label, and sends it off down a canal that's relatively free-flowing and going in the right direction. Oh, and one more thing—the bottles are rather small, so if you have a big message you must break it into parts labeled A,B,C, and so on, and put each part in a separate bottle. And there's no guarantee that all of those parts will take the same route or even arrive in sequential order.

You can readily imagine that as long as everyone plays by the rules, your message will get through and be put back together into one piece, even if there is nobody at all who understands the complete network. That key idea—that a network could function without any minute-by-minute overall control by a mastermind—was absolutely revolutionary when it was first suggested. The idea has proven to be much more than just a very good solution to a tough technical problem: it has become a way of thinking that explains a lot about the Internet "culture."

So, when you use Netscape Navigator to find a document in Stockholm or a picture in Mexico City, and it takes half a minute or so for it all to arrive, you can imagine it as thousands of little bottles, sedately floating your way down a maze of "cybercanals."

Who's Minding the Store?

"So who's in charge?" you might rightly ask. Well, one answer to that is "Nobody and everybody." But for all of this structure to work, it obviously takes cooperation. In practice, the people who are in charge of all the various pieces of architecture need to agree on certain common standards. The job of hashing out the technical details is largely the responsibility of the Internet Society (ISOC), established in 1992, and its various working groups, including primarily the Internet Engineering Task Force (IETF). This international group of engineers and programmers meets three times a year to hash out the myriad operational issues that surface.

In addition, the World Wide Web Consortium keeps an archive of information for Web developers and users and attempts to make sure products developed for the Web are compatible. And other groups like the Electronic Frontier Foundation fulfill a watchdog mission over issues like privacy and abuse. Once you're online you'll be able to visit the Web sites for all these groups (see Chapter 8, "Searching & Sites," for their Web addresses).

The World Wide Web

User-friendliness wasn't an issue back in the '60s when the military and the scientists wove together the first strands of what would become the Internet. If you couldn't enter something like *deroff -w detail.list | tr A-Z a-z | sort | uniq >detail.sorted* at a UNIX prompt, you didn't belong. The people who created, maintained, and used the Net were so comfortable with that kind of language, they would use it to talk to each other over the breakfast table. (*"Deroff -w the coffee machine while you're up, would you, dear?"*)

There was absolutely no need for user-friendliness until large numbers of users outside the university system came along. That's why all the great strides down the road to the "ultimate killer app" have been taken in this decade, the '90s.

The World Wide Web is certainly one of those strides. Once it became possible to instantly access hundreds of thousands of documents all over the world, it was only logical to think about skipping lightly from one related document to the next without laborious search-and-find operations. The World Wide Web made that possible by means of "hypertext."

Hypertext was an idea waiting to happen ever since the first writer created the first footnote. This is how it works: Say you're helping your child devise a science project. She's interested in spiders, so that's a start. You go together to the library and find a book on spiders. As you're bravely scanning descriptions of horrible tarantulas, your young genius finds an interesting section about spiders who eat their own mates or young. That sparks an interest in cannibalism among insects. You notice a footnote reference to a book about cannibalism in insects. So you pull down that book, find the appropriate section, and as you're reading you become interested in the curious habits of praying mantises. Here's something you might find in your own backyard to use for an experiment (and something a little friendlier than a tarantula). So you follow yet another bibliographic reference to a book on praying mantises.

If you were using the World Wide Web, all of this running back and forth to library shelves, jumping from book to book, would be made very easy for you. In the initial document on spiders you might see a "hypertext link" to cannibalism in insects—i.e., "cannibalism in insects" would appear highlighted in color in the text. By clicking on the highlighted link, you would go directly to the referenced document. From there, you might follow another hypertext link to "praying mantises." Whenever you find anything you want to keep, you can save it to a file on your own computer. It isn't even necessary to know the location of documents you obtain this way—the address is embedded in the text. Obviously, though, you have to have a starting point. And perhaps we should just add that, although a spider is a highly appropriate topic for the Web, the Web is just as comfortable dealing with Hollywood movies, State Legislatures, great restaurants, and paintball tournaments.

Now let's say you could click on a picture of a female praying mantis and watch it devour its mate in a short video. You might also press an audio button to hear her crunch, crunch, crunch (if you really wanted to). Now you've gone beyond hypertext to hypermedia.

Once it became possible to transmit not only text but pictures and audio and video files (and now even animation) and PC technology reached the stage where they could easily be displayed, the Web—as you can see in Figure 1-2—truly became hypermedia.

So we reach the point where we are today, when computer industry titans slug it out with Hollywood moguls on the business pages of newspapers every morning to see who will be the first to deliver to you full-scale home videos, among other things, by a click of the mouse.

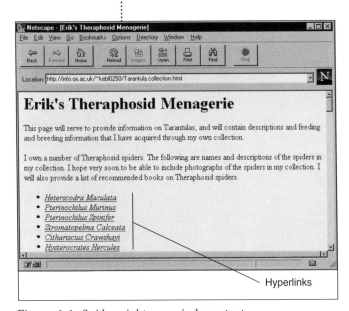

Figure 1-1: *Spider nightmares in hypertext— a collection in Oxford, England.*

What's a Web Page?

You'll hear lots of references to "Web pages" in Net talk. The term can be confusing to a newcomer. A Web page is merely a document designed to be accessed and read over the World Wide Web. It must have an address in a recognized format—the URL, or Uniform Resource Locator—that enables computers all over the world to locate it. Each Web page has its own unique URL. The term "page" arises naturally because of the visual similarity of a Web document onscreen to a magazine page. However, there are important differences to bear in mind, apart from the obvious one: these so-called pages have no fixed width, height, weight, or physical location. A Web page is actually a data document that has been encoded in ways very similar to typesetting, using a simple code language called HTML (HyperText Markup Language). The code says things like "put a picture here," "make this a header," and "start a paragraph here." It also includes codes that say "put a link here to another document."

Figure 1-2: *A NASA historical site that offers links to text, data, images, audio, and video.*

All of this code is meant to be interpreted and presented to your screen by a "Web browser." It's your Web browser, as much as the code embedded in the page itself, that actually tells your computer how to display the encoded information (the font to display text in, the screen layout to use) and that in turn is, to a certain extent, under your personal control. Netscape Navigator is one of several Web browsers currently in use on the Web, but due to its ability to incorporate many other resources on the Web, it has become the most versatile and popular browser. Estimates run as high as 80 percent of Web surfers who now use Netscape Navigator. And because of its superior display features, many Web pages are designed specifically with Navigator in mind.

The more "traditional" stuff of the Internet—FTP and WAIS, Usenet and Telnet, and the Gopher—has not gone away. It keeps on growing, and actually much of it can be read by Web software. In the early days of the Web, it could be said (and it was) that the Web was not so much a new part of the Internet as a new way of looking at what was there all the time. With the proliferation of pages specifically designed for Web browsing, that no longer holds true. But, certainly, nobody thinks we are anywhere close to being able to do away with the information that's cataloged in the more traditional ways. On the contrary, there's a clear trend for the graphical Web browsers to include more and more of those other Internet access tools wrapped in ever fancier and friendlier packages. Netscape Navigator is squarely in the mainstream of that trend.

Netscape Navigator: Your Window on the Web

When Samuel Morse invented the telegraph and made it possible for stations throughout a railroad's network to get instant information about the running of the trains, people didn't say: "Yeah, sure, this may look good right now. But just wait until the telephone comes out. It'll make this collection of wires and keys look like junk overnight." No, obviously the natural reaction to any advance is to rejoice in its benefits and to think that, in the words of the song from *Oklahoma!*, ". . . they've gone about as fer as they can go."

So it was with NCSA Mosaic, which was such an utterly different view of the Internet that it really seemed to be the be-all and end-all. Wow! In-line pictures! Wow!! Instant movies!! Wow!!! Clickable hypertext links!!! WOW!!!! It would have sold like hotcakes had it not been the product of a United States Government lab, the National Center for

Who or What Is Mozilla?   Users of Mosaic and lurkers around the Usenet groups devoted to Web developments may have picked up occasional references to a Web browser named "Mozilla" or to the "Mozilla DTD." Mozilla was the name the young programmers who designed Mosaic originally gave to their next-generation browser while they were developing it.

When Netscape Communications Corporation took over the project, the pet name in the programming department was squelched by the marketing department. But Mozilla survives as an appropriate moniker for the green dragon who occasionally appears on Netscape informational pages (see Figure 1-3). And the Mozilla DTD is the form of HTML (HyperText Markup Language) recognized by Netscape Navigator, which includes some Netscape-specific extensions.

Supercomputing Applications (NCSA) in Illinois. As it is, Uncle Sam does not deal in hotcakes, and the software is free to anyone who can figure out how to download it.

But certain entrepreneurs, who do deal in hot cakes, looked at the "gold rush" of people downloading Mosaic and thought "Hmm . . . maybe if we improved on this and put it on the market . . ."

Netscape Communications Corporation started by hiring away most of the young computer whizzes who, as undergraduates at the University of Illinois at Urbana-Champaign, had designed Mosaic. They set them to work designing a new Web browser that would not just cruise the Web but would become an all-inclusive Internet package. Netscape Navigator 2.0 has not only accomplished the original design aims, but has surpassed them by incorporating new features like up-and-coming multimedia applications. In the next chapter we'll tell you how to get started with Netscape Navigator so you can join the next wave of the Internet evolution.

Figure 1-3: *Mozilla in a whimsical mood.*

The Deluxe Internet Package

Netscape Navigator is a full-featured Web browser, which means that it is designed to operate as your principal, if not only, interface with the Internet. If you are already an experienced Internaut, you may have favorite software programs for certain operations, such as reading Usenet news or sending and receiving e-mail. You may, of course, elect to continue using these programs. But it will be possible to do all of these operations within Netscape Navigator itself, including:

- Accessing and viewing Web pages posted anywhere in the world.

- Sending and receiving e-mail to or from anywhere in the world.

- Downloading and saving text, picture, audio, and video files to your own computer.

- Reading and posting to Usenet newsgroups.

- Viewing images (in .GIF, .JPEG, and other formats) using Navigator's built-in viewer or a helper application of your choice.

- Playing audio files using Navigator's own NAPLAYER or your own application (or real-time audio by installing the application RealAudio).

- Playing animated video files using helper applications like MPEGPlay or QuickTime.

- Searching the Internet using Gopher, WAIS, Archie, Veronica, and a whole new generation of Web searchers.

- Downloading files from publicly accessible FTP sites. Also, sending files by FTP to remote computers.

Moving On

First, a quick review of the terms we've thrown at you in this chapter. For others you're not familiar with that aren't covered here, please check the Glossary at the back of this book.

- The **Internet** is a worldwide collection of computers that communicate with one another over cables, satellites, optical fibers, and phones—literally, the whole hardware mass.

- The **World Wide Web**, or **WWW**, is a system designed to access documents online over the Internet. The Web makes it possible to read and exchange text, images, sound, and video.

- **Hypertext** and **hypermedia** are what the Web uses to link related documents, allowing you to follow connections from one document to the next. Hypermedia is a more appropriate term when links are to audio and video files.

- A **Web page** is a document designed to be read over the World Wide Web, written with embedded codes for display instructions.

- **HTML**, or **HyperText Markup Language**, is the coding Web documents or pages use to tell a Web browser how to display a text file.

- **URL**, or **Uniform Resource Locator**, is the address of a file posted on the Web. It tells your Web browser on what machine to find the file and provides the full file pathway.

- A **Web browser** is a program that allows you to explore the Web. Netscape Navigator is designed not only to read and display Web documents but to be a full-featured interface for most operations you might want to do on the Internet.

Now put down your pencil, turn on your computer, and get ready. We're about to take a trip on a silicon chip into the future of the information age.

GETTING STARTED

If you're already Net-savvy, it's a safe bet that Chapter 1 didn't delay you long—and that's fine with us. So now that we're all up to speed, we can start to get organized.

In the style of the latest, most up-to-date software, Netscape Navigator is a breeze to set up, pretty much installing itself on your system. But first you need to pay attention to a few details in getting your system ready to operate.

In this chapter we'll tell you what you need to run Netscape Navigator, and how to install it on your computer and set some basic preferences. We'll also tell you how to get upgrades as they become available by FTP, as well as some of the other applications you can use to enhance your Web browsing experience. Then we'll fire up the engines, give you a quick look at the Web pages where you can learn more about Netscape and the Web, and launch you on your first around-the-world cruise on the World Wide Web.

Necessary Connections

Although it's perfectly possible to set up Netscape Navigator to use with local files in your own computer or network, to browse the World Wide Web with Netscape Navigator you will need an Internet connection. If you work for or have access to the computer facilities at a large business, educational institution, or other organization you may already have a direct Internet connection through that organization. If, like many people, you're setting up for your own home use, you'll need to get yourself configured through a private Internet Service Provider (ISP) or one of the large commercial online services that offer full Internet access.

Determining whether a commercial online service or private ISP is best for you may depend on how much time you intend to spend online, what you intend to use your connection for, and how much of the extra stuff a commercial service provides you might use. It is possible to configure Netscape Navigator to work with several of the commercial online service providers. Check in the Internet forums and information areas to see if this is possible. You'll need to download and configure the service's own Winsock to use with Navigator, and you'll probably find it easier to use the 16-bit version of Navigator rather than the 32-bit version. The Internet user forums and message areas with advice from other users are usually the best places to go for help in configuring your service for this.

If you're going the independent route, what you'll need is either a SLIP (Serial Line Internet Protocol) or PPP (Point-to-Point Protocol) connection, and they're getting cheaper and easier to set up every day. Many private ISPs now offer a complete kit of all the software you need to get set up on the Web, preconfigured for their system. The kit will usually include some version of Netscape Navigator and a TCP/IP

Peter Kaminski's List of Internet Service Providers You can obtain an up-to-date list of Internet service providers by sending an e-mail message to info-deli-server@pdial.com with the message **Send PDIAL.** You can also get this by FTP at **ftp.best.com/pub/kaminski** (add **ftp://** to the front of this address if you're using a Web browser). If you're currently not on the Net, have a connected friend get the list for you. Figure 2-1 shows the Web page that has the same data files as the FTP site.

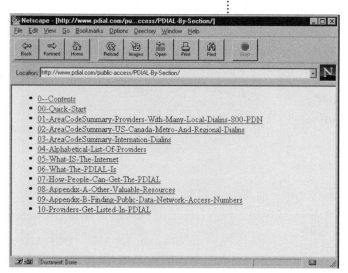

Figure 2-1: *Part of Peter Kaminski's PDIAL database of ISPs.*

stack/dialer to make your connection to the Internet. If you're shopping for a provider, you might ask about this and, all other things being equal, choose one who will go this extra step for you. If the version of Netscape Navigator provided is earlier than 2.0, it will be easy to upgrade it once you're installed.

If you choose a provider that does not offer this service, there are still several easy solutions. The Netscape Navigator Personal Edition comes with its own connection software package, which can make your life a lot easier. Several popular book/software packages such as *The Windows Internet Tour Guide* and the *Internet Membership Kit* (both by Ventana) also provide all the software you need for a SLIP/PPP connection and a lot of other helpful guidance to the Internet at large.

No matter what your provider, you may need a little patience to get set up the first time. It sometimes takes several trial-and-error attempts at setting things up before you have your communications package running smoothly. Your sysadmin (if you have one) or the sysop or help desk with your online service should be able to guide you through this process—they know their system better than you'll ever need to. It is outside the scope of this book to go into the details of configuring your system for communications since there are too many variations to cover. But we'll try to point you in the right direction for what you'll need.

Your TCP/IP Stack

You need a TCP/IP stack, also called a Winsock, to make your connection to the Internet. This program acts as an intermediary—dialing your access provider and managing the data exchange between your computer and the Internet.

If you're using Windows 95, Windows NT or have used another Web browser before, you should already have a Winsock that will work for Netscape Navigator, although you may have to check to make sure the Winsock and the Navigator version you have are compatible. To run the 32-bit version of Navigator you need a 32-bit Winsock. If you have a 16-bit Winsock and don't feel like upsetting the apple cart, use the 16-bit Navigator. Windows 95 will run either, but things will be a lot faster at 32-bits. If you're using a commercial online service, make sure your version of Navigator matches the Winsock the service provides. (You can set up with a different Winsock but you'll find configuring a bit more difficult.)

Windows 95 Setup

To use the TCP/IP stack included in Windows 95 to dial in to a private service provider, you must first install these Windows 95 components:

- Client for Microsoft Networks
- Microsoft Dial-up Adapter
- Microsoft TCP/IP

If you're on a local area network (LAN) you'll need the Network Adapter instead of the Microsoft Dial-up Adapter. Install these from the Networks area of your Control Panel. Click Add, then from Client choose Microsoft; from Protocol choose TCP/IP; from Adapter choose Dial-up Adapter. Figure 2-2 shows how your Network setup should look after you've installed these components.

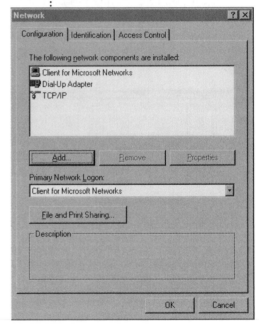

Figure 2-2: *Windows 95 Network dialog with all Internet components installed.*

To configure the TCP/IP client for your Internet connection, highlight this item and click on Properties. We wish we could tell you exactly what to put in all the confusing boxes here, but it will depend on your service provider and you'll have to get the straight scoop from there. An example of one part of the configuration is shown in Figure 2-3. The most important part is the IP address—the Internet Protocol—and it's a four-part numerical code which identifies the server's computer to the rest of the Internet. You may be assigned your own IP address for your personal use or your server may assign you one at random each time you log in.

After you've installed and configured the Microsoft TCP/IP you'll need to reboot, then open the My Computer icon and double-click on Dial-Up Networking. Select "Make New Connection" to create a connection icon for your provider. You'll need to provide the phone number for your service and configure the dialer for your modem. If your modem was already installed when you installed Windows 95, it's a good bet that the software is already set up for your particular modem.

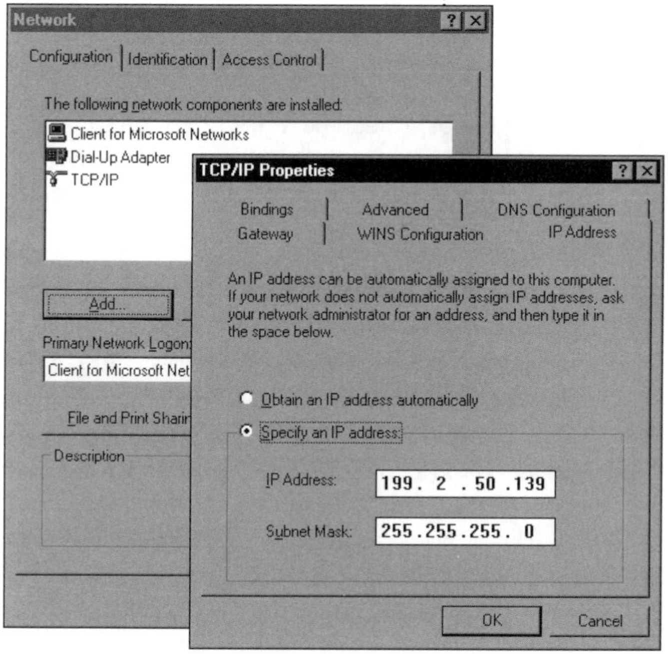

A good instruction guide for configuring the Windows 95 Dial-Up Networking to access your own service is *The Windows 95 TCP/IP Setup How-To FAQ* by Michael Rose. It's posted on the Web at: **http://www.aa.net/~pcd/slp95faq.html** and is also available by FTP from: **ftp.idirect.com/pub/win95/slp95faq.faq**.

Figure 2-3: *Your IP address: the most important part of the TCP/IP setup process.*

New versions of the document are also available at the newsgroups **comp.os.ms-windows.misc** and **comp.os.mswindows.advocacy**. See if you can get your access provider or an online friend to get it for you if you're having trouble.

Windows 3.1 & Windows for Workgroups

If you're using Windows 3.1 or Windows for Workgroups, you must use the 16-bit version of Netscape Navigator and you'll need to acquire a separate 16-bit Winsock package. There are several that will work and they're commonly available on the Internet. In addition, if you are running Win32s on your system, which you might have installed to use a previous version of Navigator or Mosaic, see the sidebar entitled "Win32s & Netscape Navigator" for another precaution.

A simple and highly reliable TCP/IP stack that works well for Windows 3.1 and Windows for Workgroups is Trumpet Winsock, a shareware product developed by Peter Tattam of the University of Tasmania. You can download the latest version at: **ftp.trumpet.com.au/winsock/**.

Other Winsocks that will work include Microsoft's WFW (Wolverine) for Windows for Workgroups, which can be obtained by FTP from: **ftp.microsoft.com/peropsys/windows/public/tcpip**. If you're using a Web browser, add **ftp://** to the front of the address.

Some other Winsocks that have been tested and will work fine are FTP Software's PC/TCP, NetManage, Microsoft NT, and Network TeleSystems (NTS).

If you don't have the right version of Navigator or need a new Winsock, you can get everything you need online by anonymous FTP or from your access provider. FTP instructions are included later in this chapter in the "Downloading Netscape Navigator" section.

Win32s & Netscape Navigator If you're running version 1.15 or below of Win32s, you'll need to either upgrade to version 1.2 or higher or remove the program entirely before you install Netscape Navigator. To find out what version you have of Win32s, check the WIN32S.INI file in your Windows system directory. In Windows for Workgroups, select the WIN32S16.DLL file from the Windows system directory in File Manager, then choose Properties from the File menu and check the Version line.

You can obtain Win32s version 1.2 by downloading the file PW1118.EXE from the Microsoft FTP site (**ftp.microsoft.com**) or Web site (**http://www.microsoft.com**). You can also connect directly to the Microsoft Download Service with your modem and a simple communications program. Dial (206) 936-6735 to connect, then download PW1118.EXE.

To remove Win32s:

1. In the SYSTEM.INI file, in the [386Enh] section, delete the line: file: device= WINDOWS\SYSTEM\win32s\win32s.386 ➡

2. In the SYSTEM.INI file, in the [BOOT] section, remove winmm16.dll from the line:
drivers=mmsystem.dll winmm16dll.

3. From the WINDOWS\SYSTEM subdirectory delete three files: W32SYS.DLL, WIN32S16.DLL, and WIN32S.INI.

4. Delete all the files in the WINDOWS\SYSTEM\WIN32S subdirectory, then delete the subdirectory itself.

5. Restart Windows.

Downloading Netscape Navigator

The latest version of Netscape Navigator is always available online directly from Netscape Communications Corporation and a number of cooperating mirror sites. According to the license agreement for Version 2.0, the software is free for educational and nonprofit use and for evaluation by commercial users. You can get information on registering your copy and getting support once you have Navigator installed.

Note: If you've got the disk with Netscape Navigator 2.0 on it, you can skip over this section and go straight to "Unpacking and Installing Netscape Navigator." If you don't have the disk or want to get the latest program upgrade, this section's for you.

You can get a copy of Netscape Navigator by anonymous FTP with either a DOS- or Windows-based communications program or from your online service through the FTP facility. If you already have a SLIP/PPP account and have been using an earlier version of Navigator or another Web browser, you may be able to download Navigator using that browser. Just go to Netscape's home page (**http://home.netscape.com**) and follow the link.

Note: If you only have a dial-up shell account to the Internet, you can obtain Netscape Navigator using that account and set it up on your computer. However, in order to use Navigator with anything other than local files (files in your own computer or network), you will need to change your shell account to a SLIP or PPP connection. You will need a Winsock either way.

Using a Windows FTP Program

If you already have your SLIP/PPP connection and your TCP/IP software installed, you can use a Windows-based FTP program such as WS FTP to download Netscape Navigator from Netscape Communications or from one of the mirror sites listed in the sidebar.

Here's what to do:

1. Log onto your account in the usual manner.

2. Launch the FTP program and set it for a binary file transfer.

3. Type **ftp.netscape.com** in the appropriate box for Host. (If you're using a mirror site, the Host will be the part of the address before the first single slash.)

   Set your program to log in anonymously (or type **anonymous** in the User name box and your e-mail address in the Password box).

4. Choose the OK button or whatever the command is to establish the FTP connection. You'll soon be connected to the FTP server at Netscape Communications Corporation.

5. Once you're connected to the remote site, make your way through the directory structure to the appropriate directory. At Netscape Communications, this is **/netscape/windows**. With any of the mirror site addresses, everything that follows the first single slash in the FTP address is part of the directory structure. With a very long address, this is

What's All This About 16-bit & 32-bit?

Netscape Navigator version 2.0 is available as either a 16-bit or 32-bit application. You will have to decide which version is right for your computer system and Internet access.

So what does all that mean anyway? Imagine a bridge into a major hub city with 16 toll booths, eight for each direction. In the off-peak hours, 16 toll booths may be adequate to handle the traffic, but come rush hour, the booths get pretty congested and it takes a lot longer for everyone to get through. Expand to 32 booths and everyone's going to get through faster and things will run a lot smoother.

That's a fair analogy for the difference between 16-bit and 32-bit operation. The package of information that gets through at any one time is twice as large. Using 16-bit software is adequate to do the job, but when the Internet's busy—and it's getting harder to find a time when the Internet isn't busy—traffic is going to be considerably held up. 32-bit applications are more compact, more fluent, and generally faster. The wave of the future is even faster, to 64-bit, which is already possible with large Unix and Sun computer systems, but is not yet available for personal computers.

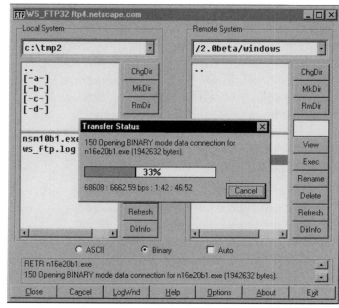

Figure 2-4: *Netscape Navigator coming down by WS FTP.*

something like winding your way down through a multi-story subterranean parking facility looking for a parking spot. When you find the right directory, you'll see a list of files available for downloading that will include both the 16-bit and 32-bit versions of Netscape Navigator, along with a license and readme file. You needn't bother downloading the license agreement or the readme file, since both will unpack as part of the main software package.

*Note: For the 32-bit version (for Windows NT and Windows 95), the file may be, for example, **n32e20n.exe**; for the 16-bit version (for Windows 3.1 or Windows for Workgroups) the file may be **n16e20n.exe**. Filenames change frequently to reflect the current version.*

6. Choose the appropriate version of Navigator and transfer it to a temporary directory on your computer using your program's Copy command. See Figure 2-4. Exit the remote site and you're ready to install Navigator on your computer.

Using Traditional FTP on a Dial-Up Account

If you have a regular dial-up shell account, you can obtain Netscape Navigator using FTP or ncftp from Netscape or one of the mirror sites (see the sidebar entitled "Netscape FTP Sites & Mirror Sites"). We'll use Netscape's FTP site for our example, but you can substitute any of the addresses listed.

Here's what to do:

1. Use your regular communications program to log onto your account.

2. At the prompt, type **ftp ftp.netscape.com** (or **ncftp ftp.netscape.com**). If you already have an FTP or ncftp prompt, you'll type **open ftp.netscape.com**.

Note: If you're using a mirror site, you'll use the part of the address before the first single slash.

3. Press Enter and you'll soon be connected to the server at Netscape Communications Corporation. If you're using FTP, log onto the remote system as "anonymous" and give your e-mail address as the password. If you're using ncftp, you won't have to (it's done for you).

4. Change the directory to the place where the current version of Netscape Navigator is available. (Everything that follows the first single slash in the FTP address is the directory structure.) At Netscape the full address might be **ftp.netscape.com/ netscape/windows/** so the command would be **cd netscape/windows**.

With some of the longer addresses in the mirror sites, finding the right directory may be a bit more labyrinthine (they sometimes change). Just remember that at any point in the directory structure, you can ask for a list of files or subdirectories by using the **ls** command. The command **ls -l** will give you a fuller description of contents, which sometimes helps in figuring out what you want.

Netscape FTP Sites & Mirror Sites Netscape maintains several FTP archives for downloading the current version of Netscape Navigator and related software. The Netscape sites are usually the first to implement changes, but any changes made to the main site are soon "reflected" by a number of mirror sites. Here's a list of the Netscape FTP sites:

ftp.netscape.com/netscape/windows
ftp2.netscape.com/netscape/windows
ftp3.netscape.com/netscape/windows
ftp4.netscape.com/netscape/windows
ftp5.netscape.com/netscape/windows
ftp6.netscape.com/netscape/windows
ftp7.netscape.com/netscape/windows

And here's a few of the mirror sites where you can get Netscape Navigator:

ftp.utdallas.edu/pub/netscape/netscape/ windows/

wuarchive.wustl.edu/packages/www/ Netscape/netscape/windows/

unicron.unomaha.edu/pub/netscape/ netscape/windows/

server.berkeley.edu/pub/netscape/windows/

ftp.micro.caltech.edu/pub/netscape/windows/
ftp.uoregon.edu/netscape/2.0beta/windows/
SunSITE.unc.edu/pub/packages/infosystems/
clients/Netscape/2.0beta/windows/

To access any of these sites with a Web browser, add **ftp://** to the beginning of the address.

You can always get an up-to-date list of mirror sites on Netscape's home page at http://home.netscape.com.

More Useful Booty: WINFTP If you don't have a Windows-based FTP program and would like one to use with your SLIP/PPP connection, there are several you can obtain online. A good 16-bit FTP program you can use with Windows 3.1 is WINFTP, which you can get by FTP at:
ftp.sunet.se/pub/pc/windows/mirror-cica/win3/winsock/.
The file to download is **winftp.zip**.

An easy-to-use, 32-bit FTP program for Windows 95 is WS FTP, which you can get at:
papa.indstate.edu/winsock-l/Windows95/FTP/.
The file to download is **ws_ftp32.zip**.

Another 32-bit program for Windows 95 is CuteFTP at:
papa.indstate.edu/winsock-l/ftp/CuteFTP.Betas/.
The file is **cftp14f2.zip**.

Add **ftp://** to the beginning of these addresses if you're using a Web browser.

---

5. Once you've accessed the right directory, the next screen you may see is a fairly fearsome warning against downloading Netscape Navigator for exportation to countries where the U.S. bans technology exports. By now you may be feeling like a spy, but don't worry. Everything you're doing is perfectly legal (as long as you're not an enemy national). Type **ls**, press Enter and you'll see a list of files available for downloading, which should include both the 16-bit and 32-bit versions of Navigator, along with a license and readme file. You needn't bother downloading the license agreement or the readme file, since both will unpack as part of the main software package.

*Note: For the 32-bit version (for Windows NT and Windows 95), the file may be, for example, **n32e20n.exe**; for the 16-bit version (for Windows 3.1 or Windows for Workgroups) the file may be **n16e20n.exe**. Filenames change frequently to reflect the current version.*

6. You'll need to tell the host computer you want the file downloaded as a binary file. Type **bin** and Enter. Then type **get n32e20.exe** (or the appropriate filename). The file will begin to transfer to your local host computer. When it is done transferring, type **quit**.

7. If you're on a dial-up account, you'll have to download the file once again from the host computer to your own home computer. Download the file into a temporary directory on your system.

Note: The procedure for downloading a file from the host computer to your own machine may differ according to the communications program you're using and the type of service you have. If you don't know how to do that, consult your communications program manual or ask your sysadmin. Also, your service may charge to store your personal files on their host system, so be sure to delete the file from your directory on the host after you've finished installing Netscape Navigator.

Unpacking & Installing Netscape Navigator

If you're installing Netscape Navigator from disk, your task will be easy: Simply insert the disk in your disk drive or CD-ROM and type **A:SETUP** (where A: is the disk drive you're using to install). Navigator will execute its setup program automatically, with just a few questions for you to answer.

If you downloaded Netscape Navigator by FTP, your task isn't much harder. If you followed instructions earlier you should have the downloaded file installed in a temporary directory. Run the **.exe** file you downloaded from Windows and it will automatically unpack to create the necessary files. Among the files it creates is SETUP.EXE. Now run SETUP.EXE to begin the installation procedure. It takes about two minutes and is shown half done in Figure 2-6.

Setup will ask you to choose a destination directory or accept the default directory by choosing Continue. If you're installing from a download, the directory in which you install Netscape Navigator must be a different directory than the one your temporary setup files are in.

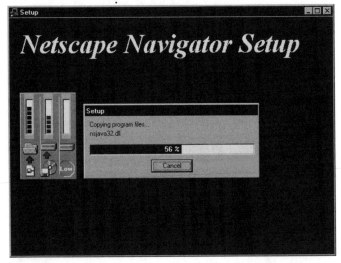

```
particular, but without limitation, none of the Software or underlying
information or technology may be downloaded or otherwise exported or
re-exported (i) into (or to a national or resident of) Cuba, Haiti,
Iraq, Libya, Yugoslavia, North Korea, Iran, or Syria or (ii) to anyone
on the US Treasury Department's list of Specially Designated Nationals
or the US Commerce Department's Table of Deny Orders.  By downloading
the Software, you are agreeing to the foregoing and you are
representing and warranting that you are not located in, under control
of, or a national or resident of any such country or on any such list.

ftp.uu.net:/networking/info-service/www/netscape
ncftp>cd windows
ftp.uu.net:/networking/info-service/www/netscape/windows
ncftp>ls -l
total 720
-rw-rw-r--   1 34       archive      2785 Nov 23 00:15 license.Z
-rw-rw-r--   1 34       archive    716395 Nov 23 00:15 ns16-094.exe
-rw-rw-r--   1 34       archive      4395 Nov 23 00:15 readme.txt
ftp.uu.net:/networking/info-service/www/netscape/windows
ncftp>bin
ftp.uu.net:/networking/info-service/www/netscape/windows
ncftp>get ns16-094.exe
Receiving file: ns16-094.exe
|55% 0                                    716395 bytes. ETA:  4:15
```

Figure 2-5: *Downloading Netscape Navigator the old-fashioned way—using ncftp in a UNIX shell.*

Figure 2-6: *Netscape Navigator 2.0 setup in progress.*

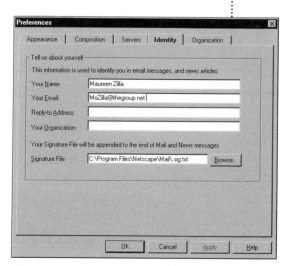

Figure 2-7: *Our* nom de Web *entered into the Identity panel.*

When the setup program finishes, you'll be ready to launch Netscape Navigator—provided you have the necessary supporting software we outlined earlier. If you installed Navigator from a temporary directory on your hard drive, you can now delete the files in the temporary directory. All of the necessary files have now been installed in their proper places on your system.

Setting Basic Preferences

You should be able to start up and begin operating Netscape Navigator immediately. Be aware, though, that some functions on the menu, such as newsgroups and mail operations, will not work until you first make the appropriate settings. Navigator's Options pull-down menu leads to a very wide choice of preferences under the headings General, Mail and News, Network, and Security. Each of these categories has several tabbed panels, and you can safely ignore almost all of them for a while.

To activate your mail and news, simply choose that menu sub-option. Two of the five Preferences tabs are of interest:

- **Identity:** Select this tab and enter your name (or your *nom de Web,* if you relish anonymity) and your personal e-mail address, as shown in Figure 2-7.

- **Servers:** Select this tab and enter the addresses of your mail host or hosts—SMTP for outgoing and POP for incoming mail (they're usually the same). Enter your NNTP news host in the box provided, as shown in Figure 2-8. If you don't know any of these, ask your sysadmin or service provider. For the time being, at least, it's safe to accept the defaults for Mail and News RC directories—we'll be explaining those in Chapter 4.

Helper Applications

For displaying audio and video files, Netscape Navigator uses "helper applications." If you have other software you use for playing movies or audio files, Navigator needs to know (and does its best to guess). The panel for setting these up is found by choosing Options from the menu bar, then General Preferences, then the Helpers tab. Again, we'll give you the skinny on this in Chapter 5, but you might like to glance at it now to see whether Navigator has correctly listed your special software.

> *Note: Netscape Navigator has its own image viewer that it uses by default, so you'll be able to operate Navigator and view World Wide Web pages without an accessory image viewer. With a graphics editor, however, you'll be able to store and manipulate images in ways that Navigator does not allow. Navigator also has its own audio player for Windows, NAPLAYER, but it will only work if your system supports it and if it's properly configured in the Helpers panel of General Preferences. You will not be able to play movie clips without a separate video application.*

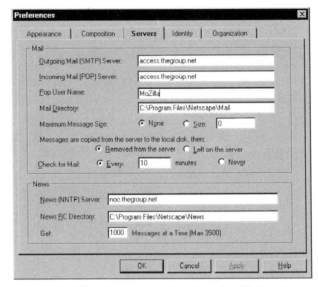

Figure 2-8: *The Servers panel needs to be filled out before we can use Netscape Navigator's e-mail and news services.*

Netscape Navigator Quick Peek

Ready to set sail on your first cruise of the World Wide Web? Here's what you should have done already:

- Set up your SLIP or PPP connection to the Internet.
- Installed a TCP/IP stack on your system and configured the dialer to dial your service.
- Downloaded and installed Netscape Navigator.

Now let's go.

1. First open Windows, if you're not already there.

2. Using your TCP/IP dialer, dial your account and log in. Once you're connected and SLIP or PPP is enabled, you can minimize the program on Windows.

3. Start Netscape Navigator by clicking on the icon or by using the Run command.

The first time you run Navigator, you will be presented with the current license agreement and be asked to accept its terms before continuing. Read, reflect, and act accordingly.

As its first act, Netscape Navigator will take you to its own Welcome page at Netscape Corporation. As it searches for its connection, you'll see the Netscape logo on the top right side of the screen start raining meteors; then you'll see the page-loading information on the bottom of the screen. All of this means that you're already sailing the Net!

Note: If the logo keeps animating and nothing's happening on the bottom of the screen except for a message saying "Trying to locate host..." you've got a connection problem. Try clicking Stop and then Reload a couple of times and if you still get no connection, you may have to talk to your sysadmin or other technical support source to get it straightened out.

Netscape Navigator in LAN or Local Mode
Netscape Navigator was designed primarily to browse the Web, but it can also be used to distribute and browse hypertext documents on a LAN, or even on a stand-alone workstation, with no Internet connection.

A problem can arise using Navigator in this way because, when properly installed for Internet use, Navigator will attempt to initiate a Winsock connection if one is not already made. Some users, particularly those with PPP connections, even find it impossible to run Navigator without establishing an Internet link.

The workaround is a little 5K file called MOZOCK.DLL. Get this file from the Netscape FTP site, in the directory unsupported/windows, and install it as WINSOCK.DLL.

The Welcome page gives you information on the latest developments with Netscape (see Figure 2-9). You'll also be given an opportunity to register your copy of Netscape Navigator, a good idea if you want to be apprised of updates.

Just above the main screen (your "Web TV") you'll see the directory buttons. Each of these takes you to another information page provided by Netscape, including an online handbook and guides to interesting sites and searching tools. You'll find a directory of FAQs (frequently asked questions) about Netscape under the Help menu at the top right of your screen. If you've got any problems to solve or questions about setup, this is the place where you're likely to find the answers.

After accessing a page, you can "back out" of it by choosing the Back button from the toolbar on the top of the screen. This will return you to the previously displayed page. If you're several pages along, you can keep backing out until you get to your original starting point. Netscape Navigator keeps a short list of where you've been—a little trail of bread crumbs through the forest—so you can follow your path back. Or choose the Home button on the toolbar and you'll return immediately to the Welcome page—unless you're ahead of the class and have already figured out how to set your own home page.

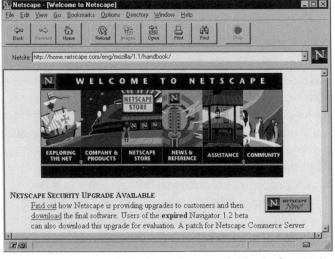

Figure 2-9: *Netscape's Welcome page: probably the first Web page you'll see.*

Using URLs

Now let's go someplace exciting and have some fun. Click on Open on the toolbar and a long rectangular Open Location window will pop up. This is like jumping into a taxi in a strange town. Like most taxi drivers, this one expects you to know where you want to go. You must enter an address in the window.

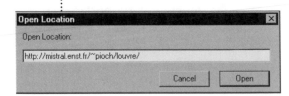

Figure 2-10: *The Open Location dialog box: We're off to Paris!*

Every Web page has its own address—its URL (Uniform Resource Locator). The window is extra-long because all the addresses on the World Wide Web are long. And, as you'll find out, addresses must be entered just right.

HOT TIP

You don't need to enter the **http://** portion of a Web page address when you want to go someplace. Netscape Navigator will automatically add it for you.

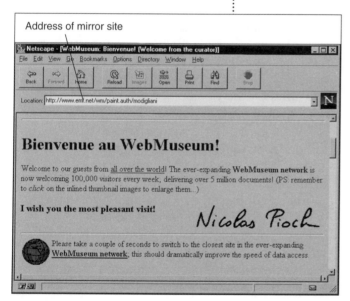

Figure 2-11: *This page by Nicholas Pioch has won many design awards—and rightly so.*

If you already have an address of a Web site you'd like to check out, you can enter it now. Then click on the Open button and you're on your way. If, like a lot of people new in town, you don't know any addresses yet, pick one that interests you from our list in Chapter 8, "Searching & Sites."Or you can try **http://mistral.enst.fr/~pioch/louvre/** as shown in Figure 2-10.

Click on Open—*et voilà! Bienvenue au WebMuseum Paris!* You have just docked along the Seine in Paris, France, where you are ready to take a tour of the collections of the Louvre, one of the most famous art museums in the world. Figure 2-11 shows the welcome page—and it also shows that we're not really in Paris after all. This Web site has become so popular that we did the polite thing and visited one of the so-called "mirror sites" that was closer to home, to relieve pressure on the main site.

Besides the fun of traveling halfway around the world in a few seconds, this Web site is a good one for illustrating the ways Web pages work. You'll notice a menu of things you can do from this Welcome page—such as a take a tour of famous paintings in the Louvre, follow links to information about various artists, visit a special exhibit, or take any of several sightseeing tours of Paris. Choose any item by clicking on the highlighted text and you'll go to another page of options.

Many of the pages contain small photos. You'll see colored borders around the pictures, which match the highlighted text links. This means you can click on the pictures and obtain larger versions of them to display on your screen. (The initial pictures are deliberately kept small so that they won't take a long time to load.) If you've got your audio system configured, you can also visit the auditorium and choose a little music to play while you stroll. Ah Paris! Wander around Paris with The WebMuseum and soon you'll be feeling like a sophisticated citizen of the Web.

Plugging Into Your Own Home Page

If you like The WebMuseum, you might like to live here for awhile. In the world of the Web anything is possible. You could choose to make The Web-Museum your home page, so that every time you start up Netscape Navigator you'll go straight to Paris.

The Ventana Visitor's Center Ventana offers an Online Companion for the *Netscape Navigator Quick Tour for Windows* as part of the Ventana Visitor's Center. The Online Companion offers all the software mentioned in the book, with the latest versions accessible as soon as they are made available, along with version change notes. There is also an online guide that will provide you with quick access to Internet resources related to this book. The *Netscape Navigator Quick Tour for Windows Online Companion* will help make this book dynamic, up-to-date, and continually useful.

The Ventana Visitor's Center can be accessed by FTP at **ftp.vmedia.com** or through the World Wide Web at **http://www.vmedia.com/vvc/index.html**.

You can also send e-mail to: **info@vmedia.com**. In the body of message, enter **send help**.

Once you have Netscape Navigator running, you can access the *Netscape Navigator Quick Tour for Windows Online Companion* at **http://www.vmedia.com/nqt.html**.

Practically speaking, this probably isn't a great idea. The WebMuseum's Web pages are such big files, and so rich in images, that you've probably noticed it takes a little while for them to load (unless you're lucky enough to be on a high-powered computer system).

But you can set up any page you choose as your home page, and you'll probably want to soon. Netscape's latest news does get a little stale after a few sessions. Many access providers have their own home pages with local information for their clients. If yours does, this might be a good place to start. Or you might prefer to go straight to some useful data page you've found—such as your morning online newspaper or the stock market report.

To set your home page, choose Options from the menu at the top of the screen. From the pull-down menu, choose General Preferences, then choose the Appearance tab (if it's not already displaying). Here you can change things like the toolbar display and link styles—you might want to fiddle with these later.

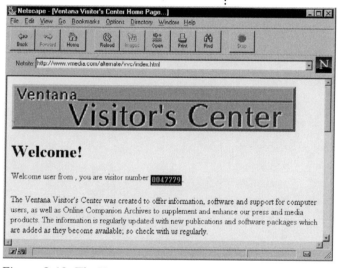

Figure 2-12: *The Ventana Visitor's Center Home Page.*

The "Start with:" option gives you the choice of starting Netscape Navigator with a blank page or a home page. Select the "Home Page Location:" radio button, then enter the address of your chosen home page in the window. Click OK and exit. You now have a new home page that will appear every time you start Navigator, or when you click on the Home button on the toolbar—until you change it again.

Later we'll show you how to devise your own home page that includes bookmarks to all your favorite sites so you can access them quickly.

Moving On

If you had a little trouble getting your dial-up connection to work, you're not alone. It seems to be a fact of life that computer communications don't work right the first time. Often they need a few rehearsals before they're ready to perform properly.

By now, though, all that downloading and installation should be behind you and you're home free. We've already introduced you to some of the features of Netscape Navigator. Next we'll tour the screen and take you through it menu by menu and button by button.

MENUS, BUTTONS & BARS

You can probably begin using Netscape Navigator right away without any further instruction, since most operations are self-explanatory. Just type in a few URLs (some good starting points are in Chapter 8) and you'll be off in no time exploring the World Wide Web on your own. Everything you really need is built in, so even without any fancy helper applications, you won't need anything extra until you're ready to tackle some gee-whiz, technowizard sites.

Because the program has so many extra features, it may take you a while to discover all the things Netscape Navigator can do for you. Once you've had a look around, you may begin to itch to download an image, send a file to a friend, retrieve a lost URL, or any of the myriad other things you can do. In this chapter, we'll talk about all those options and more that are on the menus, buttons, and bars of your Navigator screen. One of the things you'll notice as you become familiar with Navigator is that there's almost always more than one way to do something. There's a reason: When you become proficient at navigating your way around the Web, you may decide that it would be nice to have a bigger window for viewing documents. You can unclutter your screen and enlarge it by about one-quarter by making the toolbar and directory buttons—and even the URL location window—disappear. Everything you want to do can then be done using the considerably less screen-hogging menu bar—or even the keyboard, if you and your mouse are not inseparable.

We don't advise getting rid of the buttons and bars until you become familiar with all of the functions, however, and for one very good reason. Whenever a toolbar button is available to perform a function (see Figure 3-1), that's the simplest and fastest way to do it. This isn't always the case with the directory buttons, which are largely introductory. For that reason, we'll start our walkaround of the screen with the toolbar, move on to the menu bar, and end with the directory buttons. If there's more than one way of doing a particular function, we'll give you the alternatives, including menu items and keyboard commands. The recommended best way will be highlighted with asterisks.

Figure 3-1: *The nine much-used toolbar buttons.*

The Toolbar: Navigating in Netscape Navigator

The toolbar strip can be discreet or quite prominent (those big buttons are great if you're not all that dexterous with the mouse), or in between. To set its size, choose General Preferences under Options, then choose the Appearance panel. You'll see, in the Toolbars box, that you have the choice of Pictures, Text, or Pictures and Text. Just click the appropriate radio button with your mouse or use Alt-P (for Pictures), Alt-T (for Text), or Alt-C (for Pictures and Text) on the keyboard.

A text-only toolbar gains you quite a bit of screen real estate, but if you want even more you can make the toolbar go away altogether by unchecking Show Toolbar in the Options pull-down menu. We're often changing the amount of clutter at the top of our screen temporarily to suit particular Web page requirements and layouts, but if you want your decisions to carry over into subsequent Netscape Navigator sessions, use the menu choice Options/Save Options (Alt-O/S/S/Enter on the keyboard). That applies to the checklist in the Options pull-down menu only: When you make changes in the Preferences panels they will be recorded so long as you close the box with "OK" rather than "Cancel." Now, let's check out each button on the toolbar and see what it does.

Back

This button takes you back to the last Web page you were viewing. The page will almost always come from your cache, and so it will load very quickly. If you're on the first page of the session or at the beginning of your history list, this button and the menu option will both be both grayed out.

Forward

This button takes you one page forward in the history list, the record of your recent travels that Netscape Navigator keeps for you (see Figure 3-12 and the explanation under "Menu Go/History" later in this chapter). Obviously this has no meaning unless you have already done at least one Back move. Like Back, the page comes from your cache and will load quickly, and if you are at the end of your history list, the button will be grayed out.

Other Ways of Doing This
Menu Go/Back
Keyboard Alt-Left arrow
Right mouse button/Back

Other Ways of Doing This
Menu Go/Forward
Keyboard Alt-Right arrow
Right mouse button/Forward

Home

The Home button takes you immediately to your home page. At first the default will be the Netscape Navigator Welcome screen. Define whatever home page you want in the same preference panel as the toolbar display options—menu Options/General Preferences-Appearance. You can opt to start your Netscape day *tabula rasa* by picking "Blank Page," or pick "Home Page Location" and fill in the little window underneath.

Other Ways of Doing This
Menu Go/Home

HOT TIP

Your "Home Page Location" is normally expected to be the full Web address (URL) of a site such as your access provider's info page. You can, however, designate a local file, such as your own pet hyperlink list, as the "Home." If you do that, however, you need to use a weird format which turns a local path and filename into a pseudo-URL. A file called MYLINKS.HTM in the C:\NETSCAPE directory would have to be designated as:

file:///C|/NETSCAPE/MYLINKS.HTM

Note that the upper- and lower-case letters, the three forward slashes, the bar after the C—everything has to be just like we've written it or it won't work, and you'll start every day with an error message! One way to be sure of getting this right is to use Ctrl-O and bring the local page into Netscape Navigator by "browsing" for it; then select everything in the Location window and convey it to the Preference panel by copy 'n' paste.

Reload

Sometimes a Web page will only partially load into your Netscape Navigator—sometimes Navigator will confidently declare "Document done" before you've even seen *anything*. Very annoying. Sometimes a site will be so popular that it'll get gridlocked and you may need several attempts to get in (this is particularly true when Netscape has just released a new version, and you want to download it). A page you visit often may be coming from your cache, and you want to be sure you're seeing the latest version from the Net.

In all these situations, the Reload button is your friend. At its best it will restore lost graphics, get a recalcitrant page to load, or finally get through to that jammed FTP site. We guarantee nothing, however!

⌁HOT TIP

Reload operates on the page that's actually loaded to your screen, regardless of where you thought you were on your way to. Therefore, if you enter a URL in the Location window and the transfer fails completely, Reload won't help you. In that case, try putting a cursor in the Location window and hitting the Enter key.

Images

Unless you have lots of computer power at your command (and time to kill), it's a good idea to run Netscape Navigator in the "no inline images" mode on a day-to-day basis (uncheck Auto Load Images on the Options pull-down menu). It saves time downloading those page decorations that may not add a whole lot. But even the most hurried Web explorer occasionally wants (or needs) to see what the page designer intended. Figure 3-2 is an example of a page that leaves very few options (it's been improved since we captured it for the figure).

When you use the Image option, Netscape Navigator will redraw the exact same page that's already onscreen, but this time it will show all the inline images. If all you're interested in is a single image on a page, use the cursor and the right mouse button to Load This Image instead.

Open

 This is the button to use if you know exactly what URL you want to go to but it isn't yet in your bookmark list for handy fly-by-mouse. There's a first time for everything.

A dialog box appears, with a nice L-O-N-G window for you to input the URL. Even if your URL reaches the end of the box, you can still keep on entering. Be aware that URL addresses are case-sensitive and have to be entered exactly. Option buttons are Open, to tell Netscape Navigator to go where you just told it (Enter also works) and Cancel, if you think better of it. The key combination Alt-F4 also acts as Cancel.

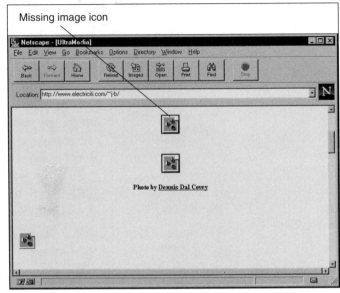

Figure 3-2: *A Web page that makes no sense without the images.*

HOT TIP

Remember, under the section on "Reload," we said that the Reload button loads the actual page you're seeing, not necessarily the page whose address is in the Location window. You can also reload the page that's in the Open Location dialog box—and that might be different from either of the above. Just bring up the window again and hit the Open button.

Other Ways of Doing This
Menu File/Open Location
Ctrl-L
Keyboard Alt-F/L

Print

Other Ways of Doing This
Menu File/Print
Keyboard Alt-F/P

This button is used to print any Web document you currently have on your screen. Choosing Print will bring up the Print dialog box, in which you can choose the number of pages you wish to print. The page will print more or less as it looks. You can preview how the document will look by selecting File/Print Preview.

Note: If you're operating in "no inline images" mode, Print will include the images, even if you don't see them on your screen.

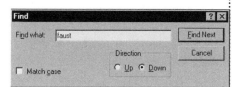

Figure 3-3: *The "Find" dialog box.*

Find

Other Ways of Doing This
Menu Edit/Find
Keyboard Ctrl-F
Keyboard Alt-E/F

This button lets you find a word or string in the current document. Don't confuse this with searching the Web for topics. What it does do is let you search a document you've accessed for a particular string—say "sea turtles" in a document on endangered species. The dialog box, shown in Figure 3-3, lets you search in either direction, and make the search case-sensitive if that's what you need.

Stop

Other Ways of Doing This
Menu Go/Stop Loading
Keyboard Esc
Keyboard Alt-G/S

As long as the Stop button is showing red, it functions to abort an attempted connection or loading of a document—usually used because it's taking too long. If you've already accessed the site, it may leave you with a partially loaded page that can be viewed and used normally so far as it goes. Sometimes you can be pleasantly surprised, as you decide to hit that Stop button and it causes quite a large proportion of the page to load before quitting. At the bottom of the partial page, Navigator thoughtfully adds the reminder, "Transfer interrupted!"

Main Menu Bar

Figure 3-4: *Netscape Navigator's nine-item menu bar.*

File

Figure 3-5: *The twelve options in the File pull-down menu.*

New Web Browser Alt-F/W

Select this option and you get a whole new Netscape Navigator to play with. This is a very neat feature, taking advantage of the bandwidth of a SLIP connection to bring you multitasking. Say you start Navigator off pulling down a page that you know is going to take time. Instead of drumming your fingers and whistling ten bars of "The Yellow Rose of Texas," you could open another window and do something else. It's also useful if you want to follow a link but keep the original page up at the same time. (See Figure 3-6.)

The maximum number of windows you can open is set in the Network-Connections preferences panel. Four is a reasonable number; six would be getting greedy (impossibly slow, on most dialup systems, but okay on a LAN). All currently-running windows are listed at the base of the "Window" pull-down menu (see Figure 3-15), and you can switch between them by clicking on that list, or by pressing Alt-Tab.

New Mail Message... Ctrl-N or Alt-F/N
Mail Document... Ctrl-M or Alt-F/M

There's not much sense in separating these two functions, since they are so similar. Both of them launch Navigator's Message Composition window for outgoing mail—the only difference is that New Mail Message makes no assumptions about the topic of your mail, whereas the Mail Document option assumes the Web page that's currently loaded is the topic, and that you probably want to send it as an attachment "as is" to your e-mail. If a Frames document is in your screen, the option changes to Mail Frame. Choose the frame you want to send by clicking in it first.

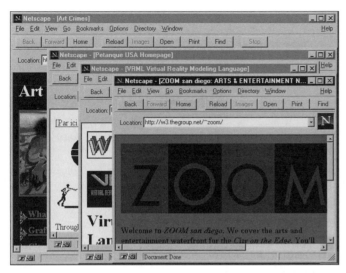

Figure 3-6: *Netscape Navigator lets you do four things at once, if you're so inclined.*

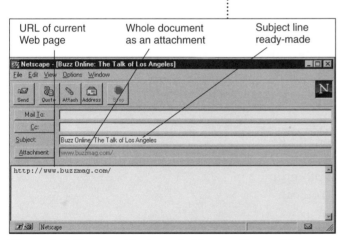

Figure 3-7: *Netscape Navigator's Message Composition window as it appears if you choose Mail Document.*

Figure 3-7 shows the Message Composition window as it appears when you opt for Mail Document. New Mail Message gets you exactly the same window but with nothing ready-made except your own address (which you don't normally see, unless you choose the Show All option from the View menu here).

We'll be explaining how to use the Message Composition window in some detail in Chapter 4, but for now just note that this window has its own File/Edit/View/Window suite of menus. You can use File/Include Original Text (keyboard Alt-F/I) to put the entire text of the current Web page into the e-mail message. Each line starts with the > symbol, like a conventional e-mail quote. The menu option Edit/Paste as Quotation (Alt-E/Q) puts the contents of the clipboard—part of the Web document that you've selected, perhaps—into the message window in the same style.

If you have a signature (.sig) file and have entered the pathway to it properly in the Options/Mail and News Preferences-Identity preferences panel, your "signature" will be appended to the text when you send. (See Chapter 4, "Mail & News," on how to make a signature file.) When you're done, there's a button for "Send." Earlier versions of Netscape Navigator had a button for "Cancel" as well—now you have to close the messaging window if you think better of this enterprise.

Warning: *Your message is going nowhere if you have not told Netscape Navigator about your e-mail arrangements in the Identity panel of Mail and News Preferences.*

Open Location...   Ctrl-L or Alt-F/L

This option brings up the long dialog box for you to enter the URL address of a Web page you want to go to.

Other Ways of Doing This
***The toolbar Open button
Direct entry to the URL window

Open File...   Ctrl-O or Alt-F/F

This option is very different from the Open Location option. If you try it, you'll see it leads to a typical Windows Open File dialog box, and the Files of Type pull-down list defaults to "*.htm." This might give you a clue as to the purpose of this feature, since a file with the extension .htm is probably a source file written in the special code known as HTML, or HyperText Markup Language. The Windows 95 version drops an even heavier hint by listing "Source files." We'll be explaining HTML in Chapter 7 of this book—but for now, all you need to know is that this option brings an HTML file from your own computer (or local network) into Navigator where it will be interpreted as a Web page. This is the so-called "local mode" used all the time by Web page authors using Navigator as an authoring tool, as well as corporations using Navigator as a LAN resource sharer.

HOT TIP

Did you know you can place a local .htm file in the Netscape Navigator window by drag-and-drop from Windows Explorer in Windows 95 or from the File Manager in Windows 3.1? You can—it's just a matter of arranging the windows appropriately.

Save As...   Ctrl-S or Alt-F/S

This is how to save a Web document that you want to preserve, manipulate, send someone for Christmas, plagiarize, or feed to your dog. It leads to the usual Windows Save As... dialog box. If a Frames document is in your screen, this option changes to Save Frame As and you can choose the frame you want to save by clicking in it first.

There may be a surprise in store for you if you do this without paying attention. The document you save defaults to an ".htm" type, and if you try to display or print it using anything other than a Web browser, it will *not* look like it did on the screen. It will have stuff like <P> and <IMG SRC> all embedded in it. Those are the HTML codes that create the look of the page. Once you save it, you'll be able to display it in Netscape Navigator as a local file using the Open File option. However, if what you're interested in is readable text to use in your word processor, use the "Save as type" pull-down list in the Save As... dialog box to give your file the extension ".txt" rather than ".htm."

Since this is the Web, what you are saving may not be text at all—it may be a picture, a sound or a movie. Make sure it has the right file extension for the file type.

Upload File

Use this option to upload a file from your computer to a remote FTP site. If this is not a public FTP site, you'll need your login and password along with the address. See Chapter 6 for more information on FTP.

Save Link As...

This is not really a menu option but it's a useful feature and this seems to be a good place to explain it. Netscape Navigator lets you save a page to a file without actually displaying it at all. This could be quite a time-saver if it's a complex document and the Net is being crabby, as it often is (especially on Fridays when every university computer goes down for weekly maintenance). Place your cursor on the hypertext link to the page, then hold down the Shift key as you click the mouse button. You will be led straight to the Save As... dialog box, and Navigator should be clever enough to know whether you are saving text, a picture, a movie, or audio.

The right mouse button also pops up a mini-menu that includes "Save this link as..." but Shift-Click is slightly more efficient.

Page Setup

Netscape has always done its best to help users create laser printouts looking as near as possible like the original Web page (if you operate a dot matrix printer, you deserve all you don't get, apparently—but that's another story).

This Page Setup screen is the latest tool for refining printouts, and it's the kind of feature you'll probably visit once only—set it and forget it.

Page Setup is shown in Figure 3-8, and perhaps the only feature that's not self-explanatory is the check box for "Beveled Lines." If you check the box, Netscape Navigator will print horizontal rules in a way that mimics the 3D rendering that they're given on screen. Otherwise, they'll be printed as solid black. Whether beveled lines are attractive or not depends mostly on how much you paid for your printer, so our advice is to try it once with and without and make an instant executive decision of your own. If someone else shares your Navigator setup, they'll probably never know they could have had it different.

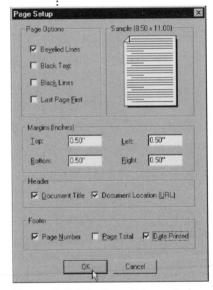

Figure 3-8: *The Page Setup window.*

Print   Alt-F/P

Other Ways of Doing This
***Use the toolbar Print button

Choosing this brings up the standard Windows Print dialog box, enabling you to change your printer setup or, more often, just go ahead and print. The page will print more or less as it looks—not as a source document. Inline images will print, too, even if you're not displaying them—provided, of course, your printer can handle them. (If you want to print source code, use File/Save As, get the file in a Notepad window and use Notepad's print function.) If a Frames document is in your screen, this option changes to Print Frame; choose the frame you want to print by clicking in it first.

Print Preview   Alt-F/V

Netscape Navigator's print preview facility is very thorough. A layout routine does its best to figure out how to present the page given your choice of fonts, the way you configured Page Setup, and the limitations of your printer. It then presents you with a picture of how the page will look, and offers buttons for (P)rint, (N)ext Page, Pre(v) Page, (T)wo Page, Zoom (I)n, Zoom (O)ut and (C)lose (see Figure 3-9). You can zoom in to as few as 21 text lines, guided by the mouse pointer toward a particular area of the page if you wish. When you're zoomed in, scroll bars allow you to look around your document.

A common problem is fitting screen lines, which may be very wide, to a printed page that typically has a line length around 66 characters. If Print Preview reveals a width problem, the solution is to return to the main display and shrink the Netscape window so the lines will wrap at a shorter length.

Figure 3-9: *One of our own information pages formatted for our HP LaserJet printer.*

Close   Ctrl-W or Alt-F/C

This option closes the Netscape Navigator window. If you have more than one Netscape window running, this may not be the end of Netscape. You'll have to close down the other windows, natch.

Exit   Alt-F/X

This is the end of Netscape Navigator, regardless of how many Netscapes you had running.

Edit

You won't be using these features very much—in normal operations they are all grayed out, with the exceptions of Select All, Find, and Find Again. And even the Find feature is more conveniently invoked with the toolbar Find button.

You can, however, select any text in the Netscape Navigator content window, no matter what size or type style, and use Copy to place it on the Windows Clipboard. At any time during the same Windows session, you can drop this text fragment into any other application having Copy/Cut/Paste features, such as a Notepad document.

These Undo/Cut/Copy/Paste/Find edit functions really come into their own, however, when you're entering text into a Web form or creating Navigator e-mail.

 HOT TIP ── . ── . ── . ── . ── . ── . ── . ── . ── . ──

You select text in the Netscape Navigator content window the same as in most Windows applications—by sweeping the mouse cursor across it as you hold down the left button. You'll see the selected text highlighted in reverse video. Sometimes, however, you need to select more than will fit on one screen. Here's the technique: Click once on the exact letter where you want to start your selection. That will lay down a "selection marker" which may or may not be visible. Now scroll on down to the end of your selected passage and click again, *this time holding down the Shift key as you click.* The whole passage will highlight and you can then slip it onto the clipboard. This process even works backwards.

Note that you don't need to go through this if what you want is the *entire* document. The menu option Edit/Select All (Ctrl-A) is available for that purpose.

View

Reload   Ctrl-R or Alt-V/R

Other Ways of Doing This
***Use the toolbar Reload button

This performs the same function as the toolbar Reload button. It re-makes the same page you are currently viewing, and gets it from the Net rather than from cache.

Reload Frame   Alt-V/C

This option reloads just one component, or cell, of a page containing multiple frames. Click in the frame you wish to reload first, then choose this option.

Load Images   Ctrl-I or Alt-V/I

Other Ways of Doing This
***Use the toolbar Images button

This is used when you are running Netscape Navigator in the "No in-line images" mode. It reloads the page adding the images.

Refresh   Alt-V/F

This has an effect very similar to Reload, but it reloads from memory rather than from disk cache or the Web. It is intended for use during HTML editing, when you might want to reload a page without seeing the effect of a change you just made to the source document.

by Document Source   Alt-V/S

Well, we've mentioned the "source document" and the "source code" a few times already. This is how you see the source—it just means the page as originally coded in the HTML convention by its author. Netscape Navigator's source display is handily color-coded to make it as easy as possible to distinguish between text and embedded coding. HTML authors—and that includes us—love this feature because it enables us to go to all the best-looking pages in the world and crib their authors' work. The Web is basically a free-for-all that makes copyright attorneys wake up screaming in the night.

If you take this option for a page that's split into several frames, the result may be a bit disappointing. You're likely to see the "top level" source code that controls the page division, but not the source of any one frame (see Figure 3-10). See the next section for a workaround.

by Document Info   Alt-V/N

Take this option, and you'll see a split-screen Netscape Navigator window. The upper half dissects the structure of the document and lists all of its components separately. Click on any line here and details of that component appear in the lower window—its security level and its temporary name in your disk cache, among other things.

Figure 3-10: *Source code window for a "frames" page—not very informative.*

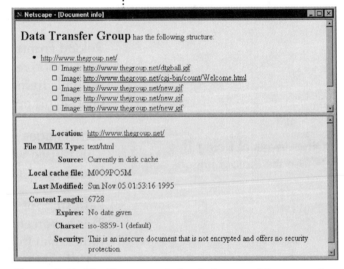

Figure 3-11: *The Document Info window—a rich source of information.*

This is the way to get at the source code of one cell in a frames page. You'll find the URL of each frame listed separately in the upper window, so you can load whatever part of the total page interests you by copying its URL to the location window, and then view its source.

 HOT TIP _.._.._.._.._.._.._.._.._.._.._.._..

The document info screen is actually a completely separate Netscape Navigator window. When you've finished with it, close it (Ctrl-W or other methods). If you use the "Back" button to return to the document itself, the Info window will be hanging around using up RAM.

_.._.._.._.._.._.._.._.._.._.._.._..

Go

The Web is so endlessly fascinating that you are very likely to go wandering off across the world for hours, especially if you're using a Web searcher to look up keywords. It would take a photographic memory to remember how on earth you got to where you are now. Navigator remembers for you—it keeps track of where you go and allows you to call up the history list at any time. The history list, like a trail of bread crumbs in the forest, is what enables you to retrace your steps safely. Generally these pages will be in your cache.

You can return to a previous page in your history list simply by clicking on it in the list, and it will be reloaded from the cache. You can also go back or forward one page at a time. The Go pull-down menu, as seen in Figure 3-12, is almost entirely concerned with navigating the history list in both directions.

Back   Alt ← or Alt-G/B

This performs the same function as the Back button on the toolbar. It takes you back to the last Web page you were viewing. If you're on the first page of the session, or at the beginning of your history list, this menu option and the toolbar button are both grayed out.

Other Ways of Doing This
***Use the toolbar Back button

Forward   Alt → or Alt-G/F

This option takes you one page forward in the history list. Obviously this has no meaning unless you've already done at least one Back move (just as "Back" has no meaning until you've done a "Forward").

Other Ways of Doing This
***Use the toolbar Forward button

Home   Alt-G/H

This takes you immediately to your home page (as defined by you in the Appearance panel under Options/General Preferences).

Other Ways of Doing This
***Use the toolbar Home button

Stop Loading   Esc or Alt-G/S

This option aborts the loading of a document and is usually used because loading is taking too long. It leaves you with a partially loaded page that can be viewed and used normally so far as it goes.

The Immediate History List

Tacked on beneath the five Go menu options is an abbreviated version of the history list itself (see Figure 3-12). You can go to any page in the list simply by clicking on that page's title. The history list can also be brought up in a window of its own, offering more options, under the "Window" pull-down menu or by pressing Ctrl-H.

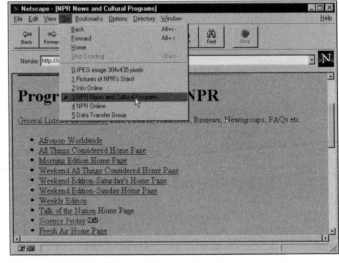

Figure 3-12: *Our history list as we've begun to explore National Public Radio's Web pages.*

Bookmarks

As you cruise the Net, you can use the Add Bookmark option to create a list of pages you might want to revisit. Once you begin to create bookmarks, a list of your bookmark pages or bookmark categories will appear here. You can go to any bookmarked page immediately by clicking on it in this list.

Creating and managing a proper hierarchy of bookmarks is a task we'll tackle in Chapter 5.

Add Bookmark   Ctrl-A or Alt-B/A

Click Add Bookmark to add the current page to your bookmark list. If you have already set up bookmark categories, it will be added to your Bookmarks listing. The bookmarks section in Chapter 5, "Bookmarks & Preferences," tells you how to set up a marker so it will add to the bookmarks folder you want it to.

Go to Bookmarks...   Ctrl-B or Alt-B/G

Choose this option and you get an extended view of your bookmark list with many editing options (see Chapter 5).

Options

Several times already in this chapter, we've referred to choices that you can make in what are called "Preferences panels." We also pointed out, at the end of Chapter 2, that there were certain preferences that were an important part of your Navigator setup.

The first four items on the Options menu lead you to subdivisions of the complex labyrinth of panels that enable you—encourage you, we might say—to customize your Netscape Navigator. We're going to cover most of these later on in Chapter 5.

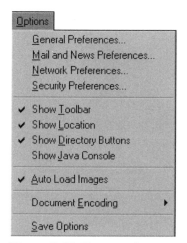

Figure 3-13: *Four toggle-check features in the Options pull-down menu.*

The second group of Options is a five-item checklist of immediate preferences that configure your screen. They're shown in Figure 3-13.

Show Toolbar   Alt-O/T

Check this feature to show the toolbar; uncheck it to remove the toolbar from your screen.

Show Location   Alt-O/L

If this feature is unchecked, the Location window below the toolbar (which shows your current URL address) goes away.

Show Directory Buttons   Alt-O/D

If this is unchecked, the directory buttons disappear, giving you a larger screen area—probably one of the first things you'll want to get rid of.

Show Java Console   Alt-O/J

This option appears in some versions of Netscape Navigator 2.0 for the benefit of Java developers. Chances are it either won't be in your copy or you can safely ignore it. For the curious, it shows the content of Java applets that may be embedded in a Web page.

Auto Load Images   Alt-O/A

As we pointed out before, it saves lots of download time to run Navigator routinely with this option unchecked, i.e., not displaying those inline images. However, certain Web pages make very little sense without the inlines—and you won't be able to tell the difference between a picture and a sound bite.

Document Encoding   Alt-O/E

This menu option allows you to set up Netscape Navigator for alphabets other than the familiar "Latin1," which is what most of us know as extended ASCII. The Web is used by people all over the world, and Latin1 may be the most common but it's not the only alphabet around. If you want to look at a Japanese Web page, it'll be gobbledegook if you haven't set the encoding to one of the Japanese options. You'll also need Japanese Windows or some Japanese enabling software.

Save Options   Alt-O/S

The way you set up your toggle checklist will be temporary, applying to your current Navigator session only, unless you choose Save Options. Preference panel decisions are saved automatically as long as you exit with "OK."

Directory

All of the options in the Directory pull-down menu take you straight to Netscape Communications Corporation where Web pages are posted to give you help and information in your explorations of the Web. Many of these menu options, seen in Figure 3-14, duplicate functions of directory buttons. Most are self-explanatory.

Netscape's Home   Alt-D/E

This is the home page Netscape sets up for you by default to get you going. Netscape Communications Corporation's home page is the place to go to find out about any new releases or the latest developments in the software.

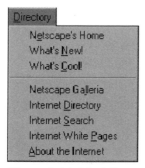

Figure 3-14: *The Directory pull-down menu.*

What's New!   Alt-D/N

This option is the same as the What's New! directory button. It is an archived monthly update of new Internet resources—with links to the latest Web pages online.

What's Cool!   Alt-D/C

This option is the same as the What's Cool! directory button. It is a collection of favorite Web pages by "the Supreme Arbiter of Taste" at Netscape Communications Corporation. Among the cool stuff is a link to The Amazing Fishcam, a "live" shot of the office fish tank (see Figure B-2 in Appendix B). Fish lovers please note the leads to other fishy sites.

Netscape Galleria   Alt-D/L

Netscape Communications Corporation maintains this page as a gallery of online services and content offerings from customers of their Netsite Communications Server and Netsite Commerce Server.

Netsite server customers can request a listing on this page by sending e-mail to: marketplace@netscape.com.

Internet Directory   Alt-D/D

This option is the same as the Net Directory directory button. It is a hyperlinked list of directories you can access to find things on the Internet. You can search for subjects, commercial services, and business sites. You can also find a directory of servers here.

Internet Search   Alt-D/S

This option is the same as the Net Search directory button. It links to various so-called "search engines," which are just a way of rapidly going through the entire Web looking for your favorite topics. You can search document titles or content by WebCrawler, Lycos, or others. We'll give you more on this in Chapter 8.

Internet White Pages Alt-D/P

Trying to find someone on the Net? Use the services listed here to locate a person or organization. Several Gopher and Telnet sites collect the e-mail addresses and names of users on the Internet that can be accessed by different search means here.

About the Internet Alt-D/A

If you're ready to study up a little further, you'll find more useful information about the Net in general here. Cocktail party experts who didn't think our Chapter 1 gave them enough small talk can crib from excerpts from *The Internet Info Guide* and The Internet Society's home page, which gives the lowdown on the history of the Net. Follow other links to FAQs and online guides.

Window

This whole pull-down menu didn't belly up to the Netscape Navigator menu bar until version 2.0 in October 1995, when several sub-functions were given their own windows to romp around in, and windowing and sub-windowing in general became more of a habit on the Web. Many Windows applications have menus with similar functions, so hopefully it won't take you too long to get used to this one. It certainly didn't faze *us* for long, once they got the bugs out!

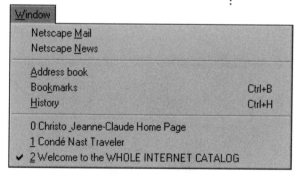

Figure 3-15: *The Window menu, with three windows running.*

Netscape Mail Alt-W/M
Netscape News Alt-W/N

The above two options open up whole new vistas, taking you into Netscape Navigator's News or Mail window, which we'll discuss in detail in Chapter 4.

Address Book   Alt-W/A

The address book displays your list of friends, business contacts, lovers, and relations in a "folders and documents" format that looks just like a file manager or bookmark list. The address book has two things in common with real life friends and relations—it takes quite a bit of management, and it's quite rewarding in the end. We'll deal with that, too, when we get down to Netscape Mail & News in Chapter 4.

Bookmarks   Ctrl-B or Alt-W/K

This takes you to your Bookmarks menu, which we cover in detail in Chapter 5.

History   Ctrl-H or Alt W/H

This nice wide window (see Figure 3-16), which is horizontally scrollable, fits those very long URL addresses that overflow the main Location window. The most recently loaded pages are at the top. Option buttons are Go to, Create Bookmark, and Close. Double-click anywhere in the list to reload that page.

Netscape Window List

Figure 3-15 showed the Window pull-down menu with three active Netscape Navigator windows listed at the bottom. When you have multiple windows running, this is a convenient way of switching between them.

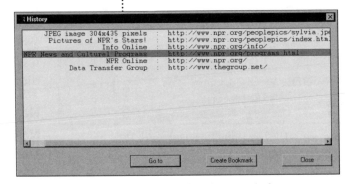

Figure 3-16: *The generously wide History window.*

Help

You'll need to be connected to the Net to use all except the first of these menu options, since the data comes from Netscape HQ. It's more up-to-date that way—in theory, at least.

About Netscape...   Alt-H/A

This brings up the Copyright notice (the lawyers advised them to put this page in). It's useful for reminding yourself which version you're using, though.

About Plug-Ins

Get information about new plug-and-play software add-ons to Netscape Navigator here. We cover some of these in Chapter 6.

Registration Information...   Alt-H/I

This leads to the User Identification Form, in which Netscape Communications Corp. can make an honest man or woman of you in 3½ minutes. They promise.

Software

Find out about program updates and additional software here.

Handbook   Alt-H/H

This is the same as the Handbook directory button. It gives you access to Netscape's online manual—a pretty complete reference guide to setting up and operating Netscape Navigator (though not as friendly as this book).

Release Notes   Alt-H/R

This tells you what version of Netscape Navigator you're running, with release notes concerning problems and fixes recently implemented. If you're having problems with some of your setups, you might check here.

Frequently Asked Questions   Alt-H/F

This is the same as the Questions directory button. Besides answering basic questions, it's a useful guide to common problems you may encounter. Look here first before badgering your sysadmin.

On Security   Alt-H/O

This is an exhaustive explanation of how Netscape (in collaboration with RSA Data Security Inc.) handles encryption of secure pages. If that's not exhaustive enough, there are more than 15 hypertext links you can follow. We'd like to tell you where the links lead, but it's hush-hush.

How to Give Feedback   Alt-H/G

This gives instructions on how to tell the Netscape designers what you think of their product, and how to report bugs you think you may have found.

How to Get Support   Alt-H/S

Info here is for business clients who want to use Netscape Navigator on a commercial scale and want to arrange for support services.

How to Create Web Services   Alt-H/C

If you're curious about how to create your own Web documents, go to this directory for references to documents that will tell you how to write WWW documents and direct you to HTML learning and style guides.

Directory Buttons

Figure 3-17: *The six directory buttons.*

The directory buttons are largely a convenience for new users—useful while you're getting acquainted but quickly outgrown. Everything on them is duplicated in the menu bar, either under Directory or Help. When you're ready to do away with them, uncheck Show Directory Buttons under Options, and gain a centimeter or so of page space.

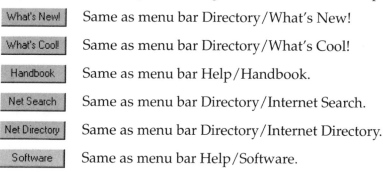

What's New! — Same as menu bar Directory/What's New!

What's Cool! — Same as menu bar Directory/What's Cool!

Handbook — Same as menu bar Help/Handbook.

Net Search — Same as menu bar Directory/Internet Search.

Net Directory — Same as menu bar Directory/Internet Directory.

Software — Same as menu bar Help/Software.

Mouse Tricks

There's one more useful button to describe, and it isn't on the screen at all. It's the one you often find under your right middle finger. Yes, that one—the right mouse button. Along about version 1.1 beta 1, somebody in the Netscape dream factory had a bright idea about how to make use of it. Click on it when pointing to a link or an inline .GIF, and up pops a very useful menu offering things you might like to do.

If you're on a hyperlink, you get these options:

- Open this (link destination)
- Add Bookmark for this Link
- New Window with this Link

- Save this Link as...
- Copy this Link Location (meaning, place its URL on the clipboard)

If you're pointing at an image, these are your choices:

- View this Image (image file name)
- Save this Image as...
- Copy this Image Location (meaning, place its URL on the clipboard)
- Load this Image (use this when you're in "No images" mode to inspect one specific image)
- Internet Shortcut (Windows 95 only)

The option, "Save Image As...," is a terrific time-saver. Towards the end of Chapter 5, we'll show you how to use it to perform acts of "cyber-larceny" that used to take quite some figuring out. (You can check out the right mouse button pop-up menu in Figure 5-10.) Also on these right button mini-menus are shortcuts to the Back and Forward options.

This can also be useful when you're cruising a site using Frames. Click in any frame and you can go Back in Frame or Forward in Frame. If you want to bookmark a document that appears in a frame, you'll have to bookmark the link to it, however, using the right mouse button option on the link.

Activity & Location Indicators

The Location Window

(Sometimes labeled the "Netsite" window.) Put a cursor in this window with your mouse and enter a URL. Netscape Navigator will go to that address as soon as you press Enter. Pop up the pull-down menu, and you get a list of the last ten URLs you entered here. Note that this does *not* mean the same thing as "the last ten URLs you visited."

Figure 3-18: *The Location Window shows you either where you are or where you're headed.*

⭕ HOT TIP

If a long and complicated URL fails, try removing everything after the basic host name plus just one slash. Then if you can get through to the host, use the URL window to add back the rest of the address, bit by bit. Or the host may offer you a link to where you want to go. It's possible the directory structure has changed or was not noted correctly.

Note: If you're entering a URL that begins **http://www** *or* **ftp://ftp**—*and that takes care of 98% of them—you can omit the protocol part and just start* **www...** *or* **ftp....** *In either case Netscape Navigator will know what you mean. This applies to the Location Window and the Open Location dialog box.*

Title Bar

The title bar is the strip at the very top between the main window buttons (see Figure 3-19). When you go to a new Web page, anything that the page's author designated as <TITLE> in the HTML code ends up in this strip.

Some titles may be so long, or your window so narrow, that they overflow. In this case, the title is truncated from the right. URLs can become exceedingly long, and the only place you can see them absolutely complete is in the box you get by selecting Window/History from the menu bar.

Progress Bar

Way down at the bottom of your Netscape window is a little strip known as the Progress bar. Actually, it's two separate bars, both of which inform you about progress in loading a Web page or a component such as a picture, movie, or sound bite. It's certainly nice to be able to look down and see "Document Received: 48% of 63K," and then "Document Done." The Thermometer bar is a comfort too, just to let you know that something's happening—but its accuracy is a bit hand-waving. It has an annoying habit of pausing just as it seems to be almost done.

The large Progress bar also displays the URL of any active link your mouse cursor is pointing at, including the name of an external image. It can be very useful to know where you will be taken if you click on that

Figure 3-19: *What appears in your title bar is under the control of the page's author.*

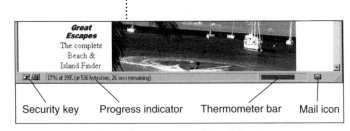

Figure 3-20: *The various components of the Netscape Navigator progress bar.*

link. At the far right of the Progress bar is the mail icon. This will change appearance by adding a little exclamation point when you have new mail (if you enable the option to have Netscape Navigator check for new mail automatically in the Servers panel of Mail and News Preferences).

Security Indicator & Color Bars

Security was one of the principal concerns of the Internet when it was first set up as a military network in the '60s. For more than a decade now, security has taken a back seat as the Net has become a DMZ. But now, as more and more merchants are using the Web to display their wares, offering potential clients the convenience of ordering by credit card, security is once again a concern.

It is now possible to produce "secure" Web pages—meaning that the text is encrypted during transmission to you, and, even more important, that any information you enter into a form is encrypted before it leaves you. You won't find many of these yet, but when you do, Netscape Navigator will signal it for you. A narrow blue bar appears immediately above the page text, and the broken-key icon at the extreme lower left will change to an unbroken key on a blue background. A security color bar is partially visible in Figure 3-21, and if you want to see what one looks like in the flesh, go to any of the Netscape Communications Corporation's pages using your Directory or Help menus (such as Welcome), then add an "s" to change the address in your URL window to begin "https://" and press return.

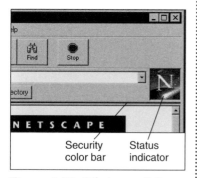

Figure 3-21: *What we call the meteor shower is officially known as the Status Indicator.*

Status Indicator (Netscape Logo)

This feature animates during loading or while trying to make a connection.

Moving On

What we've concentrated on in this chapter is the day-to-day operation of Netscape Navigator as a Web browser—which is, after all, its main claim to fame. But we perfectly well realize that we've given short shrift to some other features that may be just as important for you. "Yes, but how do I read newsgroups?" you may be yelling. Or, "Surely I can change the font style somehow?" When we give talks about Netscape somebody always asks, "How do I organize my bookmarks?"

Well, we're headed right in that direction. Chapter 4 is all about Mail and News, and Chapter 5 deals with those pesky bookmarks and those strange, strange preferences. A few of Netscape Navigator's more exotic features will have to wait until Chapter 6.

MAIL & NEWS

The Internet is not just about passive viewing of pretty Web pages, of course. Its real essence is about participation. Besides posting your own Web page (a topic we'll get to in Chapter 7, "Making Your Own Web Documents"), the principal ways you can participate are getting yourself wired for e-mail and reading and responding to the Usenet news.

Netscape simplifies your online life for you by making it possible to do both of these things from Netscape Navigator. If you have other software for these things, you'll find this a great advantage: No more switching back and forth between applications and trying to sort out software conflicts! Of course, if you're really attached to your current e-mail manager or your newsreader, you can keep them—but chances are, you'll wean yourself slowly once you see the advantages of using Netscape Navigator for everything.

In this chapter, we'll take a task-oriented approach to Netscape Navigator's Mail and News features, so you can get going on the tasks that interest you as quickly as possible. We'll also cover the organizational tools that Netscape provides to make everything run smoothly once you're all set up, like the built-in address book for mail, and sorting and filing features.

Netscape Navigator Mail

Netscape Navigator 2.0 now integrates all e-mail functions within the Web browser (previous versions only allowed outgoing, not incoming mail). Given the tendency of many Internet resources to be presented in Web format, this is a great convenience for those of us who spend most of our online time in a Web browser.

Before you can use the mail service within Netscape Navigator, you'll need to be sure Navigator knows where to go and get your mail and what to do with it.

Go to the Mail and News Preferences under Options. To get your e-mail up and going quickly, there are four items you need to enter:

- Your Outgoing Mail (SMTP) Server in the Servers panel.
- Your Incoming Mail (POP) Server in the Servers panel.
- Your POP User Name in the Servers panel.
- Your E-mail address in the Identity panel.

The SMTP server (Simple Mail Transfer Protocol) handles your outgoing mail; the POP server (Post Office Protocol) controls your incoming mail and handles the password checking. Your POP user ID is most likely the name you use in your e-mail address.

If these four blocks are completed accurately, you should be able to begin sending and receiving e-mail immediately. Other settings in the Mail and News Preferences panels are options that you can tinker with

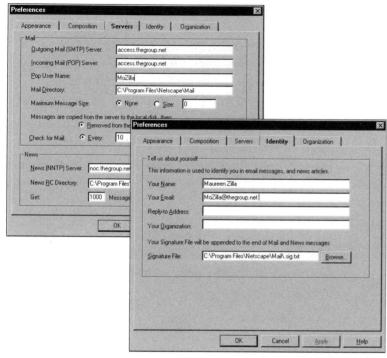

later on as you get more familiar with how the mail functions work. (See Chapter 5, "Bookmarks & Preferences," for more on Preferences panel settings.)

Windows 95 users can choose to use the Exchange Client for Mail and News by specifying that option in the Appearance panel. There's one more convenient option on the Appearance panel—if you want Navigator to automatically look for Mail and check your Newsgroups when it starts up, you can click one or both of these options.

The Mail Window

To access the full mail features of Netscape Navigator, select Window from the file menu, then Netscape Mail—or just click on the mail icon on the lower right corner of your screen.

When you first enter the Mail Window, Netscape Navigator will attempt to check with your mail server to see if there's any new mail

Figure 4-1: *The Servers panel and Identity panel of Mail and News Preferences set up for business.*

for you. You'll be asked for your password so that Navigator can retrieve the mail. If you're online, enter your password and click OK. Otherwise, just click Cancel and continue. If you don't want to be bothered with entering your password again, you can check the "Remember Mail Password" option in the Organization panel of Mail and News Preferences.

Just so you won't feel too lonely, Mozilla has kindly left your first piece of junk mail in your mailbox. Click on the envelope to open it, as we've done in Figure 4-2. (If you're lucky, it'll have more information in it than we got working with a pre-release copy—but that's another story!)

The Mail window is divided into three panes (see Figure 4-2). The top left pane shows the message folders: Inbox and Sent are the default folders for mail, plus a trash folder for deleted mail messages. You'll be able to set up your own folders to organize your mail later (see "Organizing Your Mail" later in this chapter). The top right pane shows the messages in the currently selected folder, initially the Inbox.

Next to each mail folder are two columns that display the number of Unread messages and the number of Total mail messages in each folder. Next to each mail message in the right pane you can see the sender, the subject of the mail message and the date sent. There are also two columns labeled with a red flag and a green diamond. The diamond column indicates whether the message was read or not—also note that unread messages appear in bold until read.

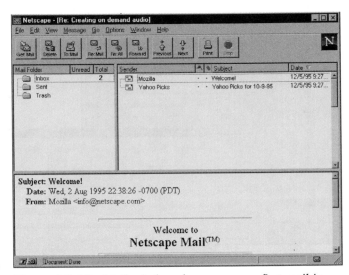

Figure 4-2: *The Mail window shows our very first mail in our Inbox.*

By clicking on the dot in this column you can mark a message unread again. (This could be useful if you're reading your boss' mail!) The flag column allows you to mark a message for your own use. Click on the dot here and a little red flag appears. You can use this as your virtual bulletin board to remind you of messages you need to reply to later, messages you need to print or re-read or forward, or anything else.

The bottom pane is the message display screen. To increase the size of this pane to read your mail, you can move the frame border with your mouse, as we're in the process of doing in Figure 4-3.

In fact, an important thing to grasp about this screen is that almost nothing in the active window area is fixed. You can move the borders of all three panes *and* collapse or expand the columns with the table headers over the top two panes. Position the mouse cursor on the border between two frames or column headings (the cursor will change shape),

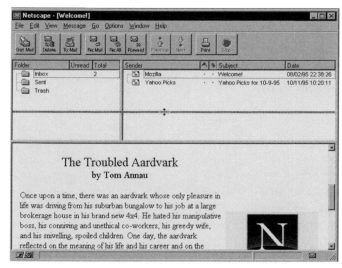

Figure 4-3: *Dragging the frame border up to resize the mail message window.*

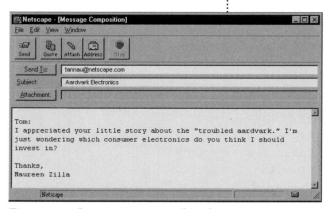

Figure 4-4: *Compose your e-mail in this Message Composition window.*

then hold down the mouse button as you drag the border. Notice the way we've readjusted the top panes of the screen in Figure 4-3, too, in order to be able to read the full dates on our mail messages. Of course, what you gain in one place, you lose in another.

Sending Mail

The next thing you'll want to do after proving to yourself you can receive mail is to try to send some. You could try mailing something to Mozilla, but he's not likely to reply. You might try sending a trial message to yourself, just to assure yourself it all works properly.

To compose an e-mail message, click on the To:Mail button, or select New Mail Message from the File menu (or Ctrl-M). The Message Composition window (see Figure 4-4) will pop into the foreground. This should be pretty self-explanatory.

Enter the e-mail address of the person you're writing to in the Send To line and the Subject of the e-mail (this is optional but polite to include). If you want the mail to go to other parties as well, enter their addresses on the Cc line. If there is no Cc line, you can add it by choosing View, then click Mail Cc. We'll deal with attachments later, so you can skip that for now. Type in your message, click on Send (or File/Send Message or press Ctrl-H). If you want to save your messages for sending later, click the Deferred Delivery option under the Options menu. The Send button will then change its appearance and will act as Send Later. Messages will be kept in the Outbox and you'll be asked if you want to send your Outbox messages when you close the mail window.

You can bring up your address book (once you get that organized) by clicking on the Address button in this screen. Click on the name you want, then click To:, Cc:, or Bcc: to transfer the address to the appropriate line in the Mail Composition window.

℧ HOT TIP

During the installation process, Netscape Navigator should set up a mail Inbox and Sent file for you in its Mail directory to keep track of incoming and outgoing mail (the Sent and Trash files may not be created until you send your first mail). However, if you get a message saying "Cannot Open FCC." when you try to send mail, go to the Composition panel of Mail and News Preferences and delete the entry in the Mail File box under the line, "By default copy outgoing messages to the file:" If you want to keep outgoing mail messages, create a new folder for outgoing mail and then put its name and path in this line.

Copying Mail to Other Recipients

You can send mail to more than one person or to a whole list of people at once.

If you don't have a Cc: line already on your composition screen, bring up the View pull-down menu. Then click on Mail Cc. A new Cc: line will appear below the Send To line where you can enter the e-mail addresses of the people you want to send to. You can enter as many as you like, separated by commas or spaces. If you want to copy the message but don't want the recipient to know who else it was sent to (in

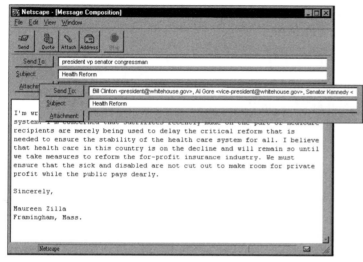

Figure 4-5: *Netscape Navigator transforms the nicknames of recipients into complete e-mail addresses using the Address Book.*

case you're sending dual love letters!), check Mail Bcc (for Blind Copies) in the View pull-down menu instead.

When you have your address book organized (see the section on "Keeping Your Address Book" later in this chapter) with the nicknames of all your regular correspondents, you can simply enter the nicknames separated by commas in the Send To:, Cc:, or Bcc: lines. See how Netscape Navigator transforms these into complete addresses in Figure 4-5.

Attaching a Document

Netscape Mail makes it easy to send any other document you may have on your computer along with your e-mail. Let's say you want to send a copy of a report to someone, along with a short e-mail note.

First, choose the New Mail button from the Netscape Mail window or File/New Mail Message (Ctrl-N) from the main Netscape window to go to the Message Composition window. Enter the appropriate Send To and Subject line information and any message you want to send along with it. Then click on the Attach button (or File/Attach File). The Attachments dialog box will appear. Click the radio button for Attach File, then browse your directories for the file and double-click on the file. You can attach as many files as you want this way (within reason!).

When you have the filename(s) in the Attachment window, click OK. The file will appear in the Attachment window in the Mail Composition window. Send your e-mail in the usual way and the attached file will go along with it as a separate file.

Note that you can choose to send the file As Is (in its original format) or Convert to Plain Text from the Attachment dialog. Since attached files are not part of the e-mail message, they can be in other formats besides text (.txt) files. An attached file might be a Word document (.doc), a WordPerfect file (.wp) or a Postscript file (.ps), for example. Recipients will be able to open and read the file using the appropriate software on their computer.

Appending a Signature File

Many e-mail regulars have signature files, which they use to sign all their correspondence easily and quickly. This can be very useful if you typically like to include information at the bottom of your correspondence, like your title, organization, address, phone number, or a pithy saying. If you have a signature file you needn't type all this information in every time.

First you have to make the signature file. This should be a simple ASCII text file. Use your Windows Notepad to compose your signature, then save it as *sig.txt*. If you save this in the Mail subdirectory of Netscape Navigator's main directory, put a period in front of the filename (.sig.txt) so that Navigator will know not to treat it as a mail folder. (It could be anywhere on your computer, but in any case you'll have to remember the path.)

Now you have to tell Netscape Navigator that you want it appended to all your messages. Go to the Identity panel of the Mail and News Preferences. Note that you can access this directly from the Mail window if you want. Choose Options/Mail and News Preferences, then the Identity tab. In the win-

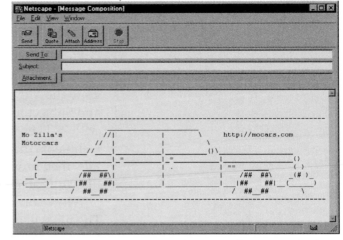

Figure 4-6: *A fancy ASCII art signature file appears in the Message Composition screen ready for input.*

dow for Signature File, enter the filename with its full path. This might be, for example, C:\Netscape\Mail\.sig.txt.

To prove that it's working now, choose New Mail. When the Message Composition screen comes up, your signature file should appear in the text area of the screen, ready for you to type your message in above it. (See Figure 4-6.)

Signature files can get quite fancy. Since you're limited to a text file, you can't insert any special fonts or formatting, but you can be a little artistic with what's known as "ASCII art." These are designs you can make using the punctuation and other characters (like the asterisk and ampersand) on your keyboard. We've used a rather flowery example in Figure 4-6. (Netscape chided us for exceeding the recommended four lines for a sig file, but we did it anyway.)

HOT TIP

If you include the URL of a Web page in your signature file, or elsewhere in your mail message, Netscape Navigator will automatically turn this into a hypertext link. Anyone who receives your mail with Navigator will be able to immediately access your Web page by clicking on the link in your mail message.

Decoding ROT13 Messages

A common method of scrambling text for e-mail is ROT13 encoding. This merely shifts the message text by 13 characters, rendering it unreadable gibberish, unless you can perform astounding feats of mental agility and convert it back in your head. Or if, like most of us bears of very little brain, you have a program to do it for you. Why you might be receiving messages like this is your own private business (please don't tell us, we don't want to know!), but here's how you do it: To unscramble any scrambled message you receive, choose Unscramble (ROT13) from the View menu in the main Mail Window when you have the message in the screen.

Quick Mail Options

For outgoing mail, you needn't bring up the full Netscape Mail window. Just choose New Mail Message from the File menu (Ctrl-N). This takes you directly into the Message Composition window. Enter your e-mail message, and just click on Send when you're done. If you're online, it'll go off immediately. If you're not online, save it to send later by clicking Later.

If you want to refer to or include the text of a Web document currently on your screen, use the Mail Document option instead—just below New Mail Message on the File pull-down menu (or Ctrl-M). The URL of the current page will automatically be included in the message window and the Subject line will default to the title of the Web page (this is illustrated in Figure 3-7). You can include the entire text of the document in your message by clicking the Quote button or by choosing Include Original Text from the Message Composition window's File menu. Add your own comments or edit the text as you will. When you bring the text into your e-mail message this way, the quoted text appears with angle brackets before each line to distinguish it from text you enter.

If you want to include only part of the page, you can bring only the portion you want into the screen using the Windows Clipboard:

1. Highlight the text on the screen (click at any point and hold the mouse button as you drag it over the text you want to copy, then release the mouse button).

2. Press Ctrl-C or choose Edit/Copy to copy the text to the Clipboard.

3. Bring up the Message Composition window and choose Paste as Quotation from the Edit menu. The copied text will drop into the mail window, with each line preceded by angle brackets to indicate the quote. (If you don't want the angle brackets, you can drop the text into the mail window with Ctrl-V or Edit/Paste.)

HOT TIP

A handy set of options is also available to you by way of the right mouse button. Just click on the right mouse button in the mail window while a mail message is up and you can reply to, forward, or delete that message, add the correspondent to your address book, or unscramble an encoded message.

Attaching a Web Document

Perhaps, rather than including the text of the document in your e-mail message, you'd like to attach it as a separate document, particularly if you find those angle brackets irritating. You can do this in two different ways:

- **As Is:** The document will be sent as an HTML source document, which can be displayed in the recipient's Web browser exactly as you see it on your screen.

- **Plain Text:** All HTML code will be edited out and the text of the document will be sent as a text file.

To attach a Web document, click on the Attach button in the Message Composition window. The Attachments dialog box will appear. Click on Attach Location (URL). In the next dialog box, the URL of the current document will appear in the Location (URL) line. Click on OK to include that document (or change it to the URL of a different document if you want). Back in the main Attachments dialog, choose the appropriate radio button to send the document As Is or Convert to Plain Text. See Figure 4-7.

Receiving Mail

You can check for new mail anytime you're online simply by opening the Netscape Mail window. If this is the first time you're using Mail in this session, you'll be prompted for your password. Netscape Navigator will remember your password for the rest of your online session and won't prompt you again.

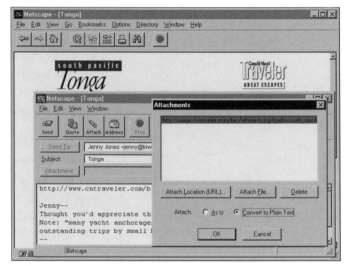

Figure 4-7: *Send a copy of a Web page in Netscape Navigator to a friend as an HTML file or a text file.*

HOT TIP

If you're worried about your mail security, it's a good idea to close down Netscape Navigator when you leave your desk. Otherwise, if you've already given your password to the mail manager, anyone will be able to download your new mail.

If you're already working in the Netscape Mail window and want to check to see if any new mail has come in, just click on the Get Mail button (or choose Get New Mail from the File menu). You can also click on the mail icon in the lower right corner of any Netscape Navigator screen to check for current mail.

You can also set up your mail service to check for new mail regularly while you're online. In the Servers panel of Mail and News Preferences, choose the radio button for "Check for Mail Every..." and specify any interval in minutes. Netscape will check the host for mail and will notify you if there's new mail with a change in the mail icon in the bottom right corner of your screen, but to avoid interrupting your tasks, it will wait until you choose to download it. Just click on the mail icon when you're ready.

Replying to Mail

If the message you want to reply to is open in your mail screen, you need only click on the Reply button (or choose Message/Reply from the menu bar or press Ctrl-R). If no message is currently displayed in the content window, click on the message file you want to reply to, then choose Reply. The Message Composition window will pop up, with the Send To and Subject lines already filled out for you.

If you receive an e-mail message addressed to several recipients, you can reply to all the recipients at once using the Reply All button or Message/Reply to All (Ctrl-Shift-R).

You can change the Subject line if you want and add any other recipients using the Mail Cc: or Mail Bcc: options on the View menu. If you want to include the text of the mail you're replying to, click on the Quote button or choose File/Include Original Text and the text will be brought into the content window, with angle brackets to indicate the quoted text. If you *always* want the text of the original message to be quoted in replies, you can check the radio button for "Automatically quote original message when replying" in the Composition panel of Mail and News Preferences. Add your comments or edit the message as you like, then click Send and it's history. (See Figure 4-8.)

Forwarding Mail

You can forward any mail you've received to other correspondents quickly and easily. Simply click on the mail file you want to forward, then click on the Forward button (or choose Message/Forward from the menu bar or press Ctrl-L). The Mail Composition window will come up with everything filled out for you. The file you chose to forward will appear as an attachment. If that's the way you want it (as a separate file attached to the e-mail message), enter the Send To information, then click Send and it's off.

   If you want to forward the mail in the body of your e-mail instead, so that you can add your own comments, select File/Include Original Text and the entire contents of the chosen mail message will appear in the composition window, with angle brackets to indicate the quoted section. You should delete the filename from the Attachment line to avoid sending it twice (click on the Attachment button, hit Delete in the Attachments dialog, then OK). You can also change the Subject line, add your own comments, and send it when you're ready.

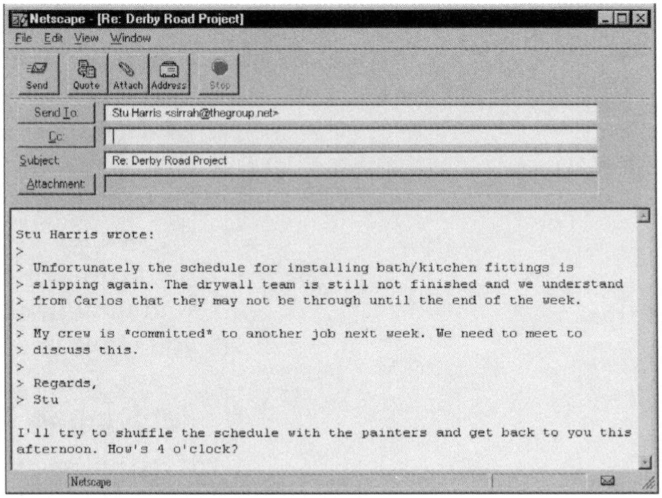

Figure 4-8: Drop the text of a message you're replying to in your Message Composition window with the Quote button and add your comments.

Organizing Your Mail

Netscape Navigator initially gives you two folders for your mail: an Inbox and a Sent folder for outgoing mail (which may be created the first time you send mail—see previous note in the section on "Sending Mail"). It's easy to add your own folders, however, and organize the mail you want to keep in nice, neat stacks. You can also display messages in different order according to your preference and use the handy "virtual bulletin board" to keep track of things to do with the mail.

Creating New Mail Folders

To create a new folder, choose "New Folder..." from the File menu. Enter the name for your new folder in the dialog box and click OK.

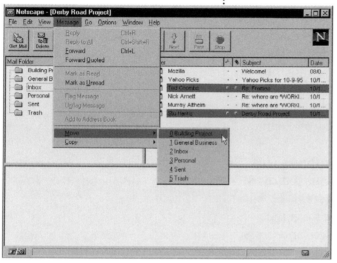

Figure 4-9: *Moving a couple of messages from the Inbox to another mail folder.*

Your new folder will appear in the Folder list. To put mail messages into this folder, you can drag and drop any message icon. You can also do this by clicking on a message or several messages at once (hold down Ctrl while clicking on successive messages), then choose Move from the Message menu to display the names of your folders. Choose the one you want to move the message to (see Figure 4-9). You can copy a message to another folder (leaving the original where it is) the same way. Just choose Copy instead of Move from the Message menu.

There are several options for sorting the messages in any folder as well. Choose Sort from the View menu, and then check whether you want mail sorted by Date, by Subject, or by Sender. Sorting by date causes messages to be displayed chronologically, earliest to latest. Sorting by Subject or Sender displays messages in alphabetical order.

Marking Messages

To mark messages for future action, use the flag column in the mail message pane. Just click on the dot in the flag column next to the message and a red flag will appear to serve as your reminder.

Use the diamond column to mark messages as unread in the same way (useful if you didn't have time to get through it all before lunch). The message will appear again in bold and a green dot will show up in the diamond column as a reminder.

You can do both of these operations from the Message menu, too, if you prefer. Under the Options menu you can also choose to Show Only Unread Messages instead of Show All Messages.

Deleting Messages & Cleaning Out Folders

Netscape Navigator also creates a Trash file for you when you delete mail. You can delete mail by moving a message to the Trash file. The simplest way, though, is to highlight the message file, then press the Delete key or click on the Delete button. In case you might want to rummage around in the trash for something you need, Mail remains in the Trash folder until you actually delete it a second time by choosing Empty Trash Folder from the File menu.

Clean out your folders of old messages by using the Compress This Folder or Compress All Folders option on the File menu. This removes any old backup copies of deleted messages from your folders.

If you want to delete a mail folder, choose Delete Folder from the Edit menu. Or simply highlight the folder you want to delete and press the Delete key.

Keeping Your Address Book

Nothing will make your online communications easier than having a well-organized address book. Once you enter all your regular corre-spondents here, you'll never again need to type their e-mail addresses, and you can even shorthand the names for quick and easy entry.

To get to the address book, choose Address Book from the Window menu. From the Message Composition screen, you can press the button labeled Address for the address book. (This option is available when the cursor is on any of the addressing lines, but you can only apply your address book entries to the Send To, Cc, or Bcc lines.) The Address Book looks like an ordinary Windows file menu. You can cut, copy, paste, and move things around by drag and drop here just like you do in your Windows File Manager or Windows Explorer. But first, let's add a few names so you get the feel of how it works.

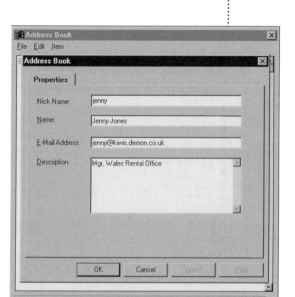

Figure 4-10: *The Properties window shows the address book information for Jenny Jones.*

Adding Names to the Address Book

From the Address Book display, choose Item, then Add User. A Properties panel appears (see Figure 4-10) with four entry areas. The first item, Nick Name, allows you to enter a nickname (or "alias" as it's often termed in online computerese) for the person. You can use a first name, a last name, initials, or a cutesy nickname here as shorthand. This can cut down many keystrokes when you're addressing mail to frequent correspondents. For example, Jenny Jones is aliased as "jenny" and so when we want to send mail to her, we just enter "jenny" in the "Send To:" line and Navigator knows who we mean. (Note: All nicknames *must* be in lowercase letters. No caps allowed!)

Enter the full name of the person and the e-mail address on the appropriate lines. In the Description box, you can enter any notes you wish to keep handy about the person. Click OK and the person is added to your address book list. You can display and edit the properties of anyone at any time by selecting Item/Properties from the menu again.

You can also add anyone from whom you've received e-mail to your Address Book by clicking on the message, then choosing Add to Address Book from the Message menu. The Properties dialog box will pop up for you to enter the rest of the information for the person.

Categorizing Your Address Book

If you have a lot of correspondents, you might want to have different lists for different things. You can categorize your address book by creating different lists. Select Add List from the Item menu and enter the properties for this list in the same way you add individual correspondents. Once you have your folder for the list, you can add people to this list. One possible advantage of keeping different lists is that you can send mail to everyone on a list at once.

To add a person to a mailing list, drag and drop the individual icon onto the mailing list folder. The original icon for the person will remain in its place and a second alias will appear in the folder. You can also delete your cast-off pals, fired business associates, or entire areas of your life with the Delete option on the Edit menu. Deleting correspondents from the main list will delete them from all other lists (Navigator will warn you of this first), but if you remove them from one mail folder, they'll remain on your main list. Figure 4-11 shows a well-ordered address book ready to do service.

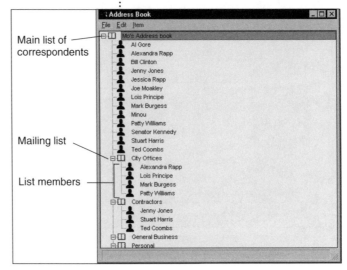

Main list of correspondents

Mailing list

List members

Figure 4-11: *A tidy Netscape Navigator Address Book ready for business.*

 HOT TIP — . — . — . — . — . — . — . — . — . — . —

Use the Nickname window in the Properties box to assign an alias to an entire mailing list. When you enter this nickname in the address line of any mail message, the mail will be sent to all the members of that list.

— . — . — . — . — . — . — . — . — . — . — . —

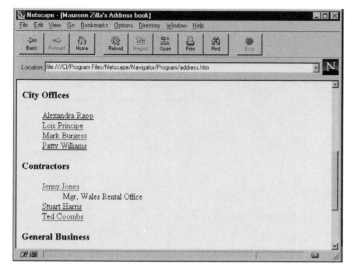

Figure 4-12: *The Address Book called up as an HTML file.*

You can manage different address books by saving your address book under a different name. Use File/Save As and enter the filename of your choice. The file will be saved as an HTML document.

To add the contents of another address book file to the current one, use the File/Import option. Navigator will warn you of any conflicts with current aliases (nicknames) as it adds the new names and will not change any of your current aliases.

You can open your address book in the regular Netscape Navigator window using the File/Open File (or Ctrl-O) option, just as you can your default ADDRESS.HTM file. Try that and you'll see the names in your address book as hypertext links on the page, along with any notes you put in the Description box. (See Figure 4-12.)

HOT TIP

Bring your address book into your regular Netscape Navigator window using the Open Local File option. Then add this file to your bookmarks. You can then view your address book and open up a ready-made mail blank addressed to someone just by clicking on their name.

Reading the Usenet News

To access Usenet News, choose the Netscape News item from the Window pull-down menu.

Before using this feature, you'll need to tell Netscape Navigator the name of your NNTP server (Network News Transport Protocol). Enter this in the News section of the Servers panel of Mail and News Preferences from the Options menu. If you're already a case-hardened Usenet freak, you may be able to use your existing NEWSRC file (it's the file that keeps track of what newsgroups you like reading and what articles you've already read). Enter the filename and path to your NEWSRC in the News RC Directory window. (See Figure 4-13.)

If you don't give it a preexisting NEWSRC file to use, the first time you go to the newsgroups, Navigator will kindly offer to create one for you. It will subscribe you to the three "newbie" newsgroups: **news.announce.newusers, news.newusers.questions**, and **news.answers**.

If this is your first time, you'll want to see the list of newsgroups available from your news server so you can choose what you want to subscribe to. Select "Show All Newsgroups" from the Options menu. The number and type of newsgroups available to you depends on the news host your server subscribes to. It's quite likely to be several thousand, though, so it will take a little time to download the list. Navigator will warn you of this, so you can go away and do something else while it goes about its task.

If you're using your old NEWSRC and have already subscribed to several newsgroups, you can choose from the Option menu to Show Subscribed Newsgroups, Show Active Newsgroups, or Show New Newsgroups. When you enter the News Window, Navigator will automatically display the subscribed newsgroups and give you updated information on the number of articles currently posted. Select Show Active Newsgroups to bring up newsgroups with new messages since

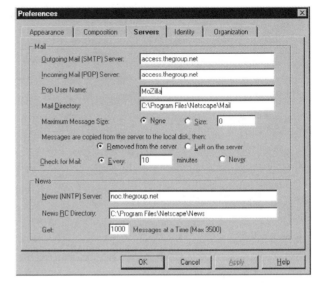

Figure 4-13: *Make sure your news (NNTP) server is entered in the Servers panel of Mail and News Preferences.*

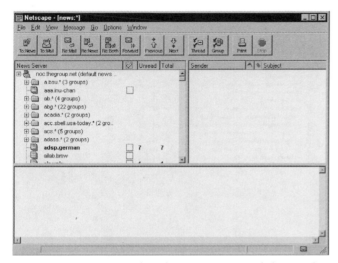

Figure 4-14: *Our news host has sent us several thousand newsgroups we can subscribe to. Where to begin?*

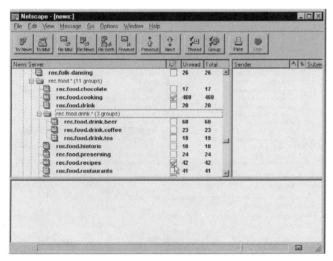

Figure 4-15: *We're subscribing to a couple of tasty newsgroups here.*

you last checked in and Show New Newsgroups to download new newsgroups added since you last looked at the list.

Subscribing to Newsgroups

Once your newsgroups listings have been downloaded from the news host, you'll have a nested list of newsgroups that looks something like Figure 4-14.

Scroll down through the list and when you find a category you're interested in, click on the folder to open it and display more. Double-click on any newsgroup to peruse the articles currently posted. When you find a newsgroup you want to subscribe to, click the cursor in the Sub box to subscribe. (See Figure 4-15.)

If you know the name of the newsgroup you want to subscribe to, just choose Add Newsgroup from the File menu and enter its name in the prompt box.

The News Window

Netscape Navigator's newsreader looks at first blush just like the Mail window. In fact, they're very much alike. The window is divided into the same three panes, although they're used slightly differently. The top left pane shows the newsgroups you're subscribed to and information about postings. Click on any one of these and the top right pane shows a list of messages posted to the group. Then click on any one of these messages and the message itself is displayed in the bottom pane. Each of these panes scrolls independently.

It's really important in the News Window to realize that you can move the borders of each frame. If you're subscribed to a newsgroup with a long name, or to several similar newsgroups, you might not be able to see all the information until you do. In Figure 4-16 we're resizing the first pane so that we can see the full names of the newsgroups at the same time as the article posting info. First, we expanded the column head by dragging and dropping the line between News Server and Sub in the header, then we resized the pane by dragging and dropping the frame border between the two top panes. In Figure 4-17, we've readjusted this again so we can see more information about the articles available in the right pane.

Reading the News

Netscape Navigator's newsreader is what's known as "threaded," meaning that all articles on the same topic are grouped together. Replies to previous postings automatically take the same Subject line and are linked, making it easy to follow the conversation and figure out who's saying what to whom about what. In Figure 4-18 you can see the outline of a couple of evolving discussions by noting the indenting and outline structure.

Start reading any article by clicking on the message icon, then go to the next unread article in this thread by clicking on the Next button. Return to the previous article by clicking Previous. These options are also available from the Go menu. You can continue through all the newsgroup postings this way.

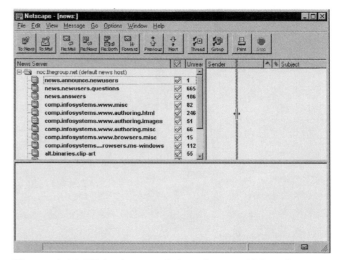

Figure 4-16: *We've increased the column width and are resizing the pane to see the full names of our newsgroups.*

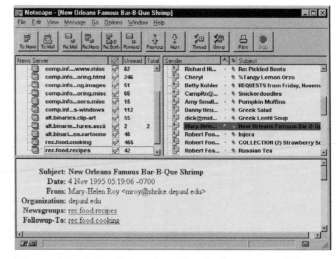

Figure 4-17: *Now that we're subscribed, we can get down to reading.*

Mark thread read   Mark all read

Chances are, however, some topics won't be of interest to you. Any time you come across a thread you're not interested in continuing, click the "Mark thread read" button (labeled Thread) to mark the entire thread as already read and the reader will skip over the rest of the articles in it. You can also choose to mark any thread as read before you start by clicking the icon for any of its articles, then clicking the "Mark thread read" button. You can mark all current articles as read with the "Mark all read" button (labeled Group).

If you want to be even pickier than that, you can mark articles using the flag column in the article listings pane. When you start to read, Next will take you to the next marked article.

Posting to Newsgroups

When you're reading the news, you can post a reply to any article currently on your screen by clicking the "Post reply" button (which is labeled Re: News). If you want to send your comments directly to the author of the current article as well, choose the "Post and reply" button (labeled Re: Both). The To: Mail button will send your comments only to the author of the article and not to the newsgroup—nice if the comments you're offering are not likely to be interesting to the group at large. You can see the difference between these buttons on the next page. All of these options are also available in the Message pull-down menu as well as the buttons.

To post an article on a new subject to the group, choose the To: News button, or New News Message from the File menu. The composition window you get for composing a newsgroup posting is identical to that

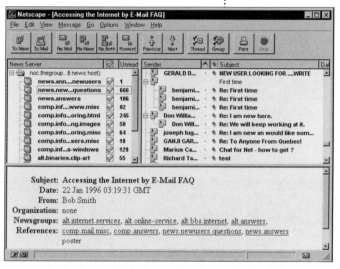

Figure 4-18: *A threaded discussion about Benjamin's "first time" is going on in this newsgroup.*

in Mail. The difference is only in the way the mail is pre-addressed. Many other options available to you in Mail are also available here. You can:

- Forward the article to someone else (Message/Forward).
- Encode or decode postings using ROT13.
- Sort articles according to date, subject, or sender (View/Sort).
- Search article text (Edit/Find).

Hypertext Reading & Posting

Another great feature is Netscape Navigator's ability to automatically interpret hypertext links and HTML formatting in news articles. We already mentioned how Netscape Navigator makes hypertext links out of URLs in a signature file. To see other examples, subscribe to one of the newsgroups that discusses the Web, like **comp.infosystems.www.misc** (you'll find Netscape announcements and bug discussions here). Many of the articles will be "signed" with a hypertext link to the author's home page, or will contain links to images, other URLs, or whatever HTML can provide.

Of course everybody thinks of newsgroups as being about trading written comments. But there are also newsgroups that deal in non-text commodities like images and audio, for instance. These groups signal their specialty by having the word "binaries" somewhere in the title. Navigator very smartly decodes binaries and displays them for you on the fly—Figure 4-19 shows a picture of a helicopter some Web artist posted viewed in the newsreading window.

Post new

Post reply

Post and reply

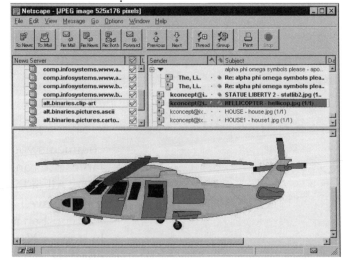

Figure 4-19: *A picture from the newsgroup alt.binaries.clip-art presented in Netscape Navigator's newsreader.*

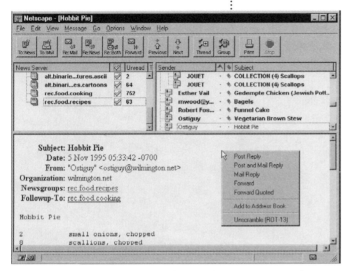

Figure 4-20: *The right mouse button brings up several convenient options while you're reading the news.*

In fact, several useful commands are available at the tip of your finger with the right mouse button. Click on any article currently in your screen and a handy set of options appears for posting, replying, or forwarding an article. (See Figure 4-20.) Similar options are available from the Mail window.

Moving On

With what you've learned in this chapter, you should be well on your way to organizing your online communications. When your Mail and News features are all set up to your liking, you'll be feeling like you've truly joined the new Information Age.

In the next chapter we'll tackle another important organizational task: fixing up your bookmarks list. As you cruise the Web and begin to accumulate more and more favorite sites, you'll want to find some way of keeping them from overflowing your screen and taking over your desk. Don't despair! Help is on its way.

BOOKMARKS &
PREFERENCES

In this chapter you'll learn how to customize Netscape Navigator for your own taste. You'll learn how to control those unruly bookmarks to keep track of your favorite places, and we'll explain how to customize the display and tailor the program to suit your system and other software you may have.

How to Use Bookmarks

Managing bookmark lists for graphical Web browsers has definitely been a hang-up. The problem is that we can all imagine what our ideal bookmark manager should be like, but for an application programmer to provide the tools you need to get from here to there is quite another matter. Netscape Navigator bookmark features, more than any other aspect of the software, have changed as the product has evolved. Fortunately, the changes have all been in the direction of improvement, and

Navigator's bookmark manager now approaches the ideal (*our* ideal, at least) quite closely. As you go through this chapter, keep in mind that your list won't look anything like the figures we've provided if you're using an out-of-date version of Navigator. Also, you're likely to encounter problems when you try to follow our instructions.

It may help at the outset to realize that all of your bookmark information is contained in a file called BOOKMARK.HTM (or anything else you may have loaded from the File menu of the Bookmarks window). Try loading this same file into the Netscape Navigator content window—press Ctrl-O to open it as a local file. Aha! Yes, as you make up your bookmark list, you are actually creating a hypertext document (see Figure 5-9 later in this chapter).

So be patient as you follow our instructions (don't expect the computer to intuit your intentions) and before very long you'll end up with the hierarchical bookmark list of your dreams.

Creating Your First Few Bookmarks

Opinions may vary about this, but our advice is to just add your first few bookmarks in haphazard fashion by going to a page you like, and using the Menu option Bookmarks/Add Bookmark (Ctrl-A or Alt-B/ A). The process happens so quickly that you won't see any evidence of your new bookmark until you click on Bookmarks in the menu bar. Then there it is, its title appended below the pull-down menu. Click on it, and you'll go right back to that page.

As you add more and more of your pet pages, you'll begin to understand the need for managing the list more logically. It doesn't take too many pet pages to overflow the screen height and make that list unusable. Figure 5-1 shows a very simple bookmark list, and Figure 5-2 shows one that's getting out of hand.

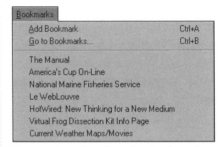

Figure 5-1: *Our first few bookmarks.*

Figure 5-2: *At about this point, we knew our bookmark list needed organizing.*

Categorizing Bookmark Lists

The first step is to group your bookmarks in categories. Open up your Bookmark window (press Ctrl-B or Alt-B/G, or choose Window/Bookmarks) and think about the categories that would be useful to you personally. In the list shown in Figure 5-3, some obvious categories would be Reference, Educational, and Magazines. The rest can be grouped as General for now.

Actually, making the groups is an exercise in managing a list of folders and documents. Notice first that you already *have* a folder-and-document list. The 21 randomly-ordered bookmarks in Figure 5-3 are a list belonging to a master folder called "Gayle and Stuart's Bookmarks." You can open and close this folder by double-clicking on it, alternately revealing and hiding its list. Practice that a few times if you want to waste a little time while giving the impression of being hard at work. Another thing to doodle with is using the mouse to highlight, or select, any bookmark in the list. Its destination URL appears in the status area. A double-click (or opting for Item/Go To Bookmark) sends Navigator off to that particular bookmarked URL.

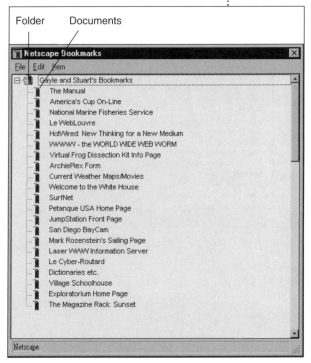

Figure 5-3: *The same list as in Figure 5-2, seen in the bookmark editing window.*

To discipline this unruly list, the task is to create four new folders, one level "down" from the master folder, called Reference, Educational, Magazines, and General. Use the mouse pointer to select the master folder. Now take the menu choice "Item/Insert Folder" (Alt-I/F). A Properties window will pop up. Simply replace the words "New Header" with "Reference" and click on "OK." It's done. Now re-select the master folder with the mouse, and go through the same process three more times. The Bookmark window will now look like Figure 5-4, with the folder list "upside down" because each new folder goes to the top. We can fix that in a jiffy.

Dragging Bookmarks into Folders

Now all you have to do is move each bookmark into its appropriate folder simply by dragging and dropping. You can even select a whole group of bookmarks scattered throughout your list by holding down the Ctrl key as you click on them, then drag the whole lot into a folder at once (be sure to release the Ctrl key, or your bookmarks will be copied, instead of moved). It's dead easy: pretty soon you'll have all your bookmarks grouped.

 HOT TIP — · — · — · — · — · — · — · — · — · — · — · —

As with almost all Windows lists, a contiguous section can be selected by clicking on the item at the top of the section, then Shift-clicking on the item at the bottom.

— · — · — · — · — · — · — · — · — · — · — · — · —

Adding Separators

Close the Bookmark window, and you'll find that what you now have is a pull-down bookmark menu that includes Reference, Educational, Magazines, or whatever else applies to your list, so that clicking on Magazines produces the Magazine list to pick from, and so on. That's what is meant by a hierarchical list (see Figure 5-5).

Now you can, if you wish, make the list slightly easier to read and use by adding separators between your folders. Return to your Bookmark window and close up all your folders by clicking on the minus symbol next to the folder (or double-clicking the folder itself). Now select each one in turn, and take the menu option Item/Insert Separator (Alt-I/S). You'll see new graphics arrive on your screen—but the effect that really matters is what then happens to your bookmark list in Navigator's main window—see Figure 5-6.

Netscape Bookmarks window:

File Edit Item

- Gayle and Stuart's Bookmarks
  - General
  - Educational
  - Magazines
  - Reference
    - The Manual
    - America's Cup On-Line
    - National Marine Fisheries Service
    - Le WebLouvre
    - HotWired: New Thinking for a New Medium
    - WWWW - the WORLD WIDE WEB WORM
    - Virtual Frog Dissection Kit Info Page
    - ArchiePlex Form
    - Current Weather Maps/Movies
    - Welcome to the White House
    - SurfNet
    - Petanque USA Home Page
    - JumpStation Front Page
    - San Diego BayCam
    - Mark Rosenstein's Sailing Page
    - Laser WWW Information Server
    - Le Cyber-Routard
    - Dictionaries etc.
    - Village Schoolhouse
    - Exploratorium Home Page

Netscape

Figure 5-4: *Four fresh folders ready to start organizing.*

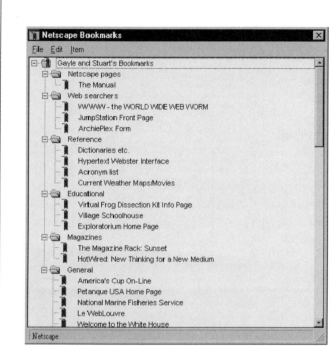

Figure 5-5: *Proper hierarchical bookmark lists.*

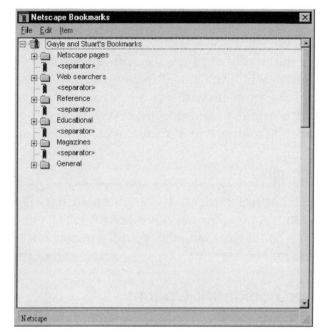

Figure 5-6: *Separators make the list easier to use.*

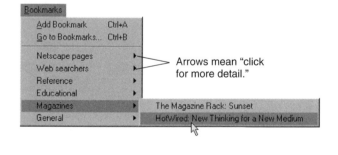

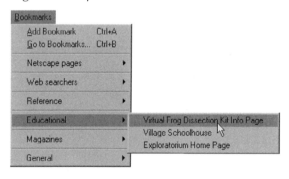

There is a downside to this process. The separators obviously take up space, and you're going to overflow the screen height quicker if you use them. Overflow is annoying because the main pull-down list is non-scrolling and bookmarks that have fallen out of the bottom of your screen can only be accessed via the Bookmark window. Figure 5-7 shows part of a superlist that solved that problem with a two-level hierarchy. That's the beauty of a folders-and-documents list—you can amuse yourself by creating folders within folders within folders *ad infinitum*.

 HOT TIP _____

If you have a particularly complex bookmark list, make a backup copy of the file BOOKMARK.HTM. Otherwise, a disk crash could wipe out all of your list management work.

Other Bookmark Options

Now that you have a decently ordered list, you can make use of a couple of other Netscape Navigator bookmark management features.

Open the Bookmark window, select any bookmark on your list and take the menu option Item/Properties (Alt-I/P). Now you can see some of the extra information that Navigator stores for you on each item in the list: its URL address, obviously, but also the date and time you created it and when you last visited it. There's also a generous-sized window in which you can write a mini-essay singing the praises of this page (see Figure 5-8). Note that although this

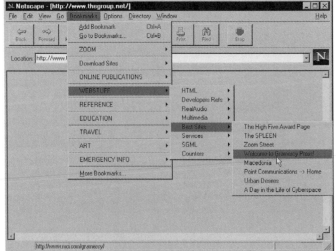

Figure 5-7: *Two-level superlists.*

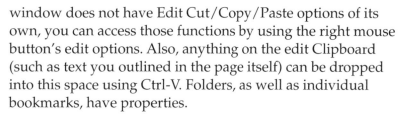

Figure 5-8: *The Properties window reveals all information about a bookmark.*

window does not have Edit Cut/Copy/Paste options of its own, you can access those functions by using the right mouse button's edit options. Also, anything on the edit Clipboard (such as text you outlined in the page itself) can be dropped into this space using Ctrl-V. Folders, as well as individual bookmarks, have properties.

Adding Fresh Bookmarks to an Ordered List

Once you have a long and well-ordered list, it's going to matter where freshly-added bookmarks end up. In the Bookmark window, you can always position a new one by selecting an existing bookmark and using the menu option Item/Insert Bookmark (Alt-I/B) to insert it right underneath.

However, that process requires you to enter the URL manually. If you're like us you'll avoid that any way they'll let you—and Netscape Navigator does, of course, let you take the easier option of just going to the Web page and hitting Ctrl-D (or choose Bookmarks/ Add New Bookmark). The interesting question then is: When you add a fresh bookmark to a nicely-ordered hierarchical list, whereabouts in the list does it end up?

Well, you may not realize it, but that's entirely under your control. At any time, one of the bookmark folders is the designated "New Bookmarks" folder—it's identified visually by one of the little book-mark icons "hidden" inside it.

That's where freshly-added bookmarks will go, and the default is the top-level folder. So if you take no action, all new bookmarks will go to the very end of the list and will have to be dragged and dropped to where you actually want them. The cool way to send your bookmarks to where you want them is to open the Bookmark window, select the appropriate folder, then choose "Item/Set to New Bookmarks Folder."

Then you can return to the main Netscape Navigator window and do your Ctrl-D add.

Possibly even cooler—but quite tricky window management—is to position a fresh bookmark by dragging a link from the Navigator window and dropping it into the list. That way you get it in *precisely* the position you want it right away.

Multiple Bookmark Lists

If you're new to this Web business, it might perhaps amaze you that there's a need for all this complexity in what is, after all, just a shopping list of interesting sites. Well, take it from us—there's *so much* that's interesting out there, no matter what your personal tastes may be, that you'll build up a fairly long list after just a month or two of Web cruising.

And speaking of personal tastes, there's one more level of complexity to come. Netscape Navigator has responded to a fairly clearly-stated demand from its users to make it easier to manage more than one bookmark list in a single computer. There are plenty of situations in which this might be helpful—his 'n' hers lists for a couple sharing a computer, separate weekday and weekend lists for the same individual, different lists for different work projects, even—although we wouldn't know about this *personally*—one "official" bookmark list and another one you might not want your boss or your wife to see.

One way Netscape Navigator has facilitated multiple lists has been simply to make it very easy to use the File/Open menu option in the bookmark window to load lists—BOOKMARK.HIM or BOOKMARK.HER to take a slightly trite example. Another way is to split a single list at the top level. We could take the list you see in Figure 5-5 and split the "Gayle and Stuart's" folder down to "Gayle's" and "Stuart's," then distribute all the other folders and bookmarks between the two.

By default, the effect this would have in the main Netscape Navigator screen is that when one of us selected the Bookmarks menu option we would see just "Gayle's" and "Stuart's," and we'd then take whatever path was appropriate. Navigator has a better way, however. Just as one folder is always designated the New Bookmarks Folder, one folder (not necessarily the same one) is designated the Bookmark Menu Folder.

That means this is the folder that will be used to make the main pull-down bookmark menu, and you designate it by selecting a folder with the mouse and choosing Item/Set to Bookmark Menu Folder.

That very inventive feature makes it highly practical to keep all your bookmarks in the same file, but categorized so as to be switchable. From Monday to Friday, say, the BIZ folder is designated. At 5 pm Friday when the factory whistle blows, out comes the TGIF bookmark folder full of all those sports and leisure sites.

Import/Export Trade in Bookmarks

We've already mentioned (more than once!) how easy it is to open any of a suite of bookmark files. The Import and Save As options on the File menu allow further manipulations. A bookmark list that's Imported rather than Opened will be added in to the current list, at the top, with all of its folders and separators intact. Bookmark file B can be added to bookmark file A, then saved as file C, and so on—and the "Save As" menu option can be important. If you spend an hour creating file C, then forget to name it, the original file A will be overwritten as soon as you close the Bookmark window.

Don't forget, too, that you always have the option to use an Import of a different kind. Figure 5-9 shows one of our lists "imported" to the main Netscape Navigator window and turned into a handy list of instant hyperlinks.

Auto Updates

The Web doesn't seem to stay the same from one day to the next. Sites come and go, sites switch their URLs—and all of this organic growth is liable to put your bookmark list out of date. A feature called Smartmarks scans either all your bookmarks or the ones you select, looking for obsolescence. Launch Smartmarks by selecting the menu option "File/What's New?" in the bookmarks menu.

Setting Special Preferences

No doubt once you get familiar with Netscape Navigator you'll want to customize it for your own use, perhaps configuring the screen to look the way you want or adding new helper applications you collect on your Web cruises. Some Preferences you have already set just to get Navigator running properly. Other settings are at the tip of your mouse finger whenever you want them. Some others you may never get interested in—and since this is a "Quick Tour" we make no claim to be giving you the whole story.

Preferences are divided into four separate categories—General, Mail and News, Network, and Security (actually, these categories and divisions change quite frequently so your version of Netscape Navigator may be somewhat different). These main categories are what you see at the top of the Options pull-down menu.

Within each category, you're expected to choose from a set of "Preferences panels" by clicking on their tabs. You can bounce around making changes all you like, but they won't take effect until you exit that group of panels with the "OK" button. Once set, all those preferences will remain that way until you come back and reset them.

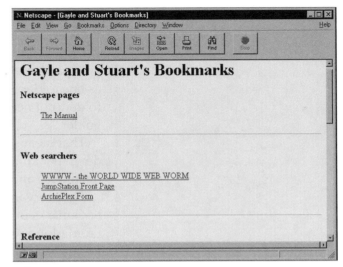

Figure 5-9: *Our bookmark list turned into a personal Web page.*

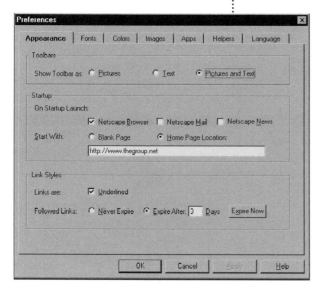

Figure 5-10: *The General-Appearance preferences panel lets you customize the look of your Netscape Navigator screen and define your home page and link styles.*

General Preferences

Here's where you come for everything to do with the actual appearance of your screen, plus the "helper applications"—other software that will work with Netscape Navigator taking on special tasks.

Appearance

You can customize the appearance of your screen in this panel (we dealt with the top two boxes, "Toolbars" and "Startup," in Chapter 3). Radio buttons allow you to select the appearance of the toolbar and whether you want Netscape Navigator to automatically launch Mail and News at startup. An input window allows you to set the URL of your home page.

The lower box (see Figure 5-10) has to do with Link Styles. Links are the hypertext words that appear in color and underlined on your screen, letting you know that a different page can be accessed by clicking on the appropriate word(s). A link might even be a picture. Once you have visited a page, its link words (or the border if it's a picture) change color—a nice feature that shows you at a glance which of the links you have already followed. In this box you decide whether you want your link words underlined, and you can select your own link colors in the Colors preference panel.

To say that the Web changes frequently is the understatement of the year—so it makes little sense for your followed links to be in a different color forever. The remaining buttons in the Link Styles box let you say how soon you want this feature to "expire," meaning revert to the same color as links you have never followed. One option is "Now," another is "Never," and you can specify any number of days in between.

Fonts

Most Web pages use a proportional font—meaning lettering like you're reading now, with the w more than three times as wide as the i. Sometimes, though, you'll come across a fixed font (also known as a monospaced font). On this panel, you can choose how to represent both types from whatever fonts you have available on your system. Typical choices are Times Roman 12-point for proportional and Courier 10-point for fixed.

If you need a larger font size to read comfortably, this is where you can choose the base font for your display.

Colors

Web page design is becoming a tricky balance between the intentions of the page designer and the preferences of the user—that's you. The original idea behind the Web was to place all control of *content* in the hands of the designer, and leave *appearance* to the user. That noble ideal has been severely eroded, and now page designers have a great deal of freedom to specify the look of their pages. That does not mean, however, that the user has lost any control—so perhaps the Web is evolving in a way that gives us the best of both worlds.

See that little check box down at the bottom, labeled "Always Use My Colors, Overriding Document" in Figure 5-11? That's basically a switch, passing control from the designer to you. Uncheck it, and the page looks as the designer intended. Check it, and you can play designer to your heart's content. You can choose the colors to display link text in and define a background color for your Netscape Navigator screen. If you want to get

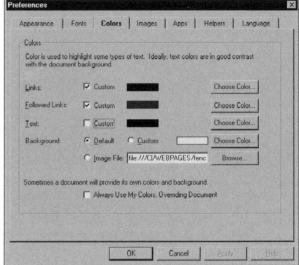

Figure 5-11: *You can choose colors for Netscape Navigator to use in this panel.*

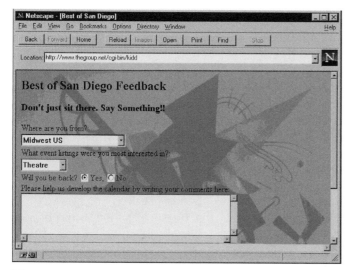

Figure 5-12: *A Kandinsky painting in .GIF form shows an ambitious use of the background option in the Colors preferences panel.*

really creative, try choosing any .GIF or .JPG you have on hand as a background. Simply put its name and path in the Image File box, and click on the radio button to the left. Navigator will present the picture (tiled as many times as needed to fill the screen) as a "desktop" background for your screen. An example of this is shown in Figure 5-12.

Apps

The Apps box is where you enter the location and name of helper applications for Telnet and TN3270 sessions (see Chapter 6), also any application you'd like to use to display (and possibly also edit, save, etc.) source code files. If you leave this box blank, source files will be displayed in Netscape Navigator's built-in window, which has no edit or save features.

HOT TIP

Netscape Navigator needs a temporary directory, where it parks various data files as it brings you the Web pages of the world. By default, it will use C:\TMP or C:\WINDOWS\TEMP if these exist on your system, or it will create its own for this purpose. A conflict can arise if other Windows applications use the same directory as their own dumping ground—and you can specify a different temporary directory in this panel.

The wise Navigator owner checks the contents of the temporary directory once in a while. Unwanted trash has a habit of building up here, taking up disk space.

Helpers

Netscape Navigator has its own built-in viewer that displays images in .GIF, .JPEG, and .XBM format. It also has its own audio player which unpacks as part of your installation. However, the viewer is not as versatile as a dedicated image-viewer, and the audio player only plays certain file types. If you're a real audiophile, you may have an application you prefer on your system or one that manages different file types. And Netscape has (so far) no built-in application to run movies or deal with the many file types you may find yourself bringing to your computer with Navigator's help.

The Helpers preference panel displays and manages a list of all these file types. By default it lists 4 types of video, 3 types of audio, 14 or so of the possible picture formats, and more than 20 other application types. If that menu is not comprehensive enough for you, you can add more of these file types—also known as "MIME Types"—by clicking on the "Create New Type" button and entering the details in a dialog box.

Your task is to go through this list, click on every file type that you think you'll ever be interested in downloading from the Net, and tell Netscape Navigator how you want to handle it. Until you make the decision, "Ask User" appears in the Action column of the File-type box.

Manipulating Kandinsky   The background of Figure 5-12 is a painting by Vasily Kandinsky called "On White II." Here's how we did it.

We grabbed the picture from the WebMuseum as a full color JPEG. (See the section on "How We Raided the Louvre" in Chapter 7.) Then, using a combination of LView Pro and Collage Image Manager, we took the liberty of rotating it 90 degrees, converting it to a 16-level gray scale .GIF, reducing its contrast, and finally boosting the gamma correction to 80. Then we just entered its path and filename in the box for Background image file in the Colors panel of General Preferences. You can do the same with whatever you'd like to see behind your Web pages: Your dream rose-covered cottage, the sled you owned as a boy, or a picture of your spouse. Whatever.

Using a largish background like this causes Navigator to pause for file loading—but only for the first screen of your session. Thereafter, the background artwork loads instantly from cache.

Your choices are:

1. Let Netscape Navigator's own software display it—only available for a minority of file types.

2. Immediately save it to a local file, leaving the display decision for later. (This is what you will want to do with .EXE and .ZIP files, to name but two.)

3. Defer a decision by declaring "Unknown: Prompt User" (that's you).

4. Launch a helper application—i.e., a whole different piece of software—that will handle this type of file. You may well want movies with file extensions .MPG, .MPEG, .MPE to be sent straight to your VMPEG player for viewing. Here's how:

Click on the "video/mpeg" line in the File-type window. See it become highlighted and the fields underneath fill in as:

File Type: video
Subtype: mpeg
Extensions: mpg, mpeg, mpe
(You may edit the extensions field).

Now bring the mouse cursor into the lower box and click on the Launch Application radio button. If you know the exact path to VMPEG, you can enter it manually in the application window—but you'll probably prefer to click on the Browse button and go find it by "hunt-and-click." Figure 5-13 shows the complete box.

We'll talk more about helper applications in Chapter 6 and point you to where you can get some useful applications by FTP.

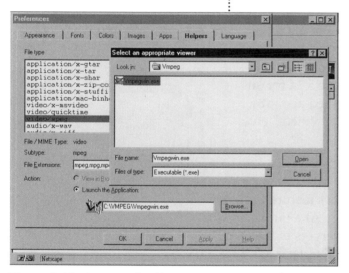

Figure 5-13: *An example of how to tell Netscape Navigator you want movies of .MPEG format to be played by VMPEG.*

Obviously, nobody can be expected to predict every single file type
they'll ever want to use with Netscape Navigator When a brand new
one does come your way, you'll be prompted to add it to your helper
applications list by filling out a little dialog box—see Figure 5-14 for an
example. In Windows 3.1, you may find yourself being asked about the
application's "type" and "subtype." Type means "image," "video," etc.,
and subtype is "jpeg," "mpeg," "rtf," and the like.

Mail & News

In order to use Netscape Navigator's mail and Usenet news features,
you need to give Netscape information about your system. At a mini-
mum, you must enter the details of your mail and news servers in the
Directories preference panel. We already covered that in Chapter 2 as
part of your initial setup. We also mentioned filling in your personal
details in the Identity panel—not quite so essential, but it sure saves a
lot of keystrokes every time you send mail. There are other options
here, not essential but interesting . . .

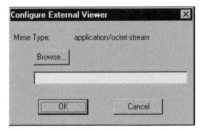

Figure 5-14: *The dialog box that
pops up when you need to use a file
type that's not on your list.*

Appearance

This panel is just a whole suite of radio buttons enabling you to select type fonts and styles for the mail and news composition window. We like to have our quoted text in italics. If you prefer to use the Windows 95 Exchange Client for mail and news, this is where you can indicate that option.

Composition

This is not the place for an erudite discussion of data transmission protocols as applied to e-mail. It's enough to know that there are many different e-mail standards in use in the world, and—guess what—they're not compatible with each other. The top-line radio buttons in this panel (see Figure 5-15) allow you to opt for either of two main systems. For routine e-mail in the U.S. and Europe, 8-bit is going to be fine. MIME-compliant is rarer but more versatile. The MIME conventions allow for things like division of the message into parts, and inclusion of a wider array of other document types, without using the 8-bit extended ASCII characters. If anyone ever says "I can only accept MIME-compliant mail," one possible answer is "Oh, OK, I'll go to my Mail Composition preferences panel and set it up for you." We can think of other answers.

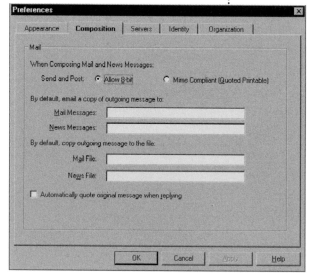

Figure 5-15: *The Composition panel allows you to keep copies of outgoing Mail/News messages automatically.*

Of more general interest are the boxes in the lower half of this panel, allowing you to set things so that your outgoing e-mail and Usenet news postings get copied either to some other person or to a "pigeonhole" file in your own computer. The world is divided into two types of people—those who couldn't bear the thought of sending a message without keeping a reference copy, and those who couldn't care less. (We represent the world faithfully—one of us cares, the other doesn't.)

If you're Type A, you're going to love this feature; but clean out that pigeonhole once in a while, do you hear?

Servers

We already covered, in Chapter 2, most of what's essential in this panel. Now we can take a second look, and refine things a bit.

First, there's another "safety" option for those cyber-packrats who like to keep copies of everything. When you fire up Netscape Navigator's Mail Window, or give it a special instruction to fetch mail from your mail server, it copies all fresh mail messages from the server to an INBOX file on your own computer—you can see its subdirectory in a window on this very panel. Now, normally your sysadmin would expect that, since they're now safely down to your inbox, you no longer need to take up space on the server, so they'd be deleted from there. Packrats will check the radio button to inhibit this process, and get occasional messages from their sysadmins asking them if they really need 60MB of old e-mail. If your server does not allow you to leave mail on the host computer, you'll get a message asking you to disable this feature when you check for mail.

As with e-mail, we covered the basics of your News setup in Chapter 2, but we skipped over the NEWSRC file. That's the data file that keeps track of the newsgroups you're subscribed to and the articles you've already read. It's perfectly safe to accept whatever this defaults to—if you've never used a Newsreader before, Netscape Navigator will create and maintain the NEWSRC file for you in that subdirectory. However, if you already use a newsreader, you have the option of telling Navigator to use an existing NEWSRC file—one that you've created for the WINVN newsreader, for instance. Simply enter the directory path, and all the subscription and catch-up information in NEWSRC will automatically appear in Navigator. From then on, Navigator and WINVN will share the same records—which is what you want.

HOT TIP

Trumpet News—one of the very best newsreaders—has a somewhat different format for its subscription record file, and it's not compatible with Netscape Navigator.

Identity

In Chapter 2, Figure 2-9 showed this panel filled in with our *Nom de Web*, and that was fine as far as it went. Now take a second look, and you'll see that under your e-mail address is a second window for a Reply-to address. Here's a bit of Netiquette that mothers will be teaching their children in the next generation—if they aren't already.

If you belong to any mailing lists—and if you don't, check the "Mail-lists" sidebar for why you should—you'll sometimes be sending e-mail to the list server for redistribution to all members of the list. If somebody else, getting your message via the list, wants to comment on it to the list in general, it's a convenience for them to be able to just hit their "Reply-to" button and off goes their comment. But the reply will simply come back to your individual e-mail box *unless* you've put the address of the list server in the Reply-to header. It's definitely considered polite to do so as you send your message—even though, in fact, sophisticated list servers do it for you—and if you're into an intensive exchange of opinion on a certain list, this is where you can put a Reply-to that will pop up in your outgoing mail automatically.

Mail-lists   Mail-lists are the most passive way of getting information out of the Internet—they can be extremely useful if you don't go crazy, and a nuisance if you do. The idea is you subscribe to some group of like-minded Morris dancers or Crystallographers, and all e-mail addressed to the Morris dancers' list server automatically goes to all the Morris dancers on the list. If you subscribe to several lists, your mailbox will have exciting things in it every day without you even having to take the trouble to look up a newsgroup. The danger, of course, is that your mailbox will get over-full and under-exciting.

One place to browse the thousands and thousands of mail-lists is the Web page maintained by Columbia Union College at http://www.cuc.edu/cgi-bin/listservform.pl. Possibly even better is the alphabetical listing at http://www.tile.net/tile/listserv/index.html.

Organization

Sorting and threading mail and news is the business of this panel. The basic question you have to ask yourself is: If a new message comes in, would I prefer it stuck on the end of the list of messages, or grouped (threaded) with other messages on the same topic? The default is threaded news, dated mail.

Network

Cache

Here's where you can specify how much memory and disk space you want to make available for the cache, according to the size of your system. The disk cache fills up very quickly and does not clear when you end your Netscape Navigator session. You can clear it with the "Clear Disk Cache Now" button. You might also use this when you need to be absolutely sure you're getting the latest version of a document rather than a possibly outdated version from cache (if you have no idea what we're talking about, check the glossary at the back of this book).

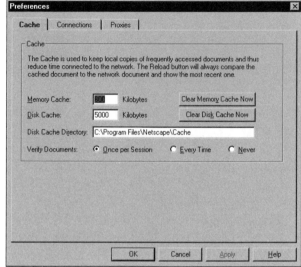

Figure 5-16: *Here's where you manage your cache.*

In general, Netscape Navigator assumes that, if a page is present in your cache, you'd rather have it served from there than from the Net. That is, after all, the whole point of a cache—to avoid the delay in downloading something you already downloaded once. If that suits you, then click on the radio button for Never after Verify Documents. That's a pretty dangerous decision, though—if you go for that you may never see the updates to your favorite Web sites. A compromise between Never and Every Time is Once per Session. That way you sacrifice a little performance in return for knowing that you're seeing pages that are pretty much up to date. Verify Every Time essentially disables the disk cache because it never gets used.

Connections

This panel allows you to specify the number of simultaneous connections you'd like—that is, how many different Netscape Navigator windows you want to be able to run at one time—and the size of the buffer for downloading them (for more windows you'll need more buffer space).

Proxies

If your Internet connection is through a large company or institution, it's possible that you're working behind what's called a firewall. This is software used to ensure the security of their system against outside hackers. If this is the case, you'll need to make use of something called a "proxy" to make your Internet connection. You needn't concern yourself with the technicalities of all this, and neither will we, since it's too variable. Just ask your sysadmin what you need to put here to make your connections for the different Internet functions you use.

Your sysadmin may make use of a script to automatically configure proxies for all users on the network. If this is the case, you can check Automatic Proxy Configuration in the Proxies panel and enter the URL of the configuration file.

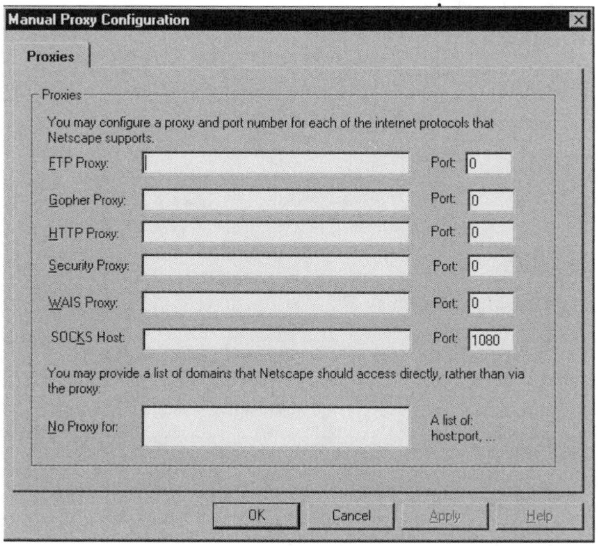

Figure 5-17: *If you're working behind a "firewall" (frequently used in large businesses to prevent unauthorized access) you'll need to fill in this box to make your Internet connections.*

Security

General

In the General panel you can specify whether you want to be advised when entering or leaving a secure page or submitting information on an insecure page. Security features are only available on specifically designed Web pages. In general you should assume information you submit on forms is insecure unless otherwise advised.

Very security-conscious users might mistrust Netscape's Java features because Java has something of a reputation as a hackers' playground. For their benefit, Netscape provides a check box that disables all Java input—the good, the bad, and the decaf.

 HOT TIP ___.___.___.___.___.___.___.___.___.

If you don't care about security and hate to be reminded every time you're doing something with security implications, uncheck all the check boxes in this panel.

Customizing Netscape Navigator for Multiple Users

With all the options available to you to customize Netscape Navigator, it's perfectly possible that multiple users on one computer will differ as to how to set it up. Tim's favorite screen colors are red, white, and blue; Jessica thinks that's garish and prefers tasteful pastels. His bookmarks are mostly computer and business-oriented; hers are educational sites she uses in her teaching job. Neither wants to sort through the other's bookmarks to find their own, and changing the BOOKMARKS file every time is a drag. And whose e-mail address gets precedence in the Mail and News box? The solution depends on whether you're running Windows 3.1 or Windows 95. For Windows 3.1, it's his and hers NETSCAPE.INI files.

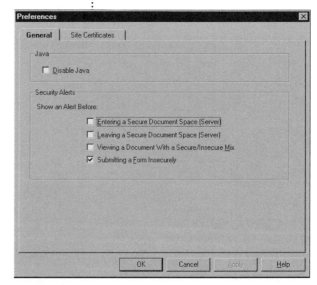

Figure 5-18: *You can choose whether you want to receive security alerts in this box.*

The NETSCAPE.INI file is the file that contains all your settings. When you make changes in the Preferences boxes, they are reflected here. To set up a personal NETSCAPE.INI file, this is what you do:

1. Make a copy of the file C:\NETSCAPE\NETSCAPE.INI in a different directory, say C:\JESS (you can choose any existing directory but it must be different than Netscape Navigator's main directory).

2. Create a second Navigator program item on your desktop.

3. For the Description line, give it a name like "Jessica's Netscape."

4. In the Command Line type: NETSCAPE -i C:\JESS\NETSCAPE.INI.

5. Navigator's own working directory, however, remains the same.

When you've added your new icon to the desktop, click on it to open Netscape Navigator and customize it to your heart's content. Now when you want to run your customized version of Navigator, just click on your own Netscape icon and it will load using your personal NETSCAPE.INI file. Any preferences you choose will be recorded only in your personal copy of that all important NETSCAPE.INI file. Perhaps most important, that includes the "Location of bookmark file" that you can define in the Preferences/Applications and Directories dialog box. So long as Jess and Tim define different bookmark files, they become personalized as well.

Windows 95 users can simply use the built-in ability to set the whole computer up for different users, entering individual log-in IDs. Access this feature via the Passwords area of the Control Panel. Having done this, most selectable features of Netscape Navigator are changed to suit the individual user—including bookmarks, cache options, address book, temporary directory, and others.

Moving On

If you're like most people, you'll continue to discover new features of Netscape Navigator as you use it. By now, besides learning how to navigate around the Web with Navigator, you should have learned how to do the following:

- Change the look of your screen to suit you, including gaining maximum screen space when you want it.

- Set up your bookmarks list and manage it as it grows.

- Customize Netscape Navigator's mail and newsreading functions for your own system and preferences.

In the next chapter we'll explore some of the fun you can have with audio, video, and multimedia helper applications. We'll also look at some of the special features you may want to use, including using Netscape Navigator to transfer files by FTP and accessing other types of files.

LAUNCHING INTO CYBERSPACE

Being inveterate travelers, the first thing we do when we arrive in a strange city is take off on a walking tour. We're usually too anxious to have a look around to bother with a map, and we've had plenty of time to peruse the travel guides at home.

You've probably felt the same way about this new cybercommunity you've just discovered. Unless you're an extremely methodical person, you probably didn't wait to get all of your helper applications installed before you took off on your first walk around the Web neighborhood.

So, in this chapter we'll take a closer look at things like movie and audio files and the helper applications you need to run them. You'll find out how to download hypermedia files and save them for offline use. We'll also talk about some other helper applications that allow you to download and view non-HTML files using Netscape Navigator and take a look at some up-and-coming applications that are being integrated into Navigator through its Java interface.

Finally, we'll take a look at those all-important Internet features like FTP, Telnet, Gopher, and Usenet that are all made available to you in a new, easy format with Netscape Navigator's interface.

The Art of Images

We all take for granted now the fact that pictures can be transferred over the Web, both embedded in Web pages and as separate files. But it wasn't so long ago that this was a real revolution. To truly appreciate it, you have to realize that this is still an evolving art on the Web. As designers and publishers climb on the Web bandwagon, and the scientists move over to make grudging room for them, the quality of art on the Web is increasing daily.

To get an overview of what's possible, take a look at the Helpers preferences panel in Netscape Navigator (under Options/General Preferences), shown in Figure 6-1. Of those beginning with "image" you'll see fourteen types with extensions like bmp, rgb, ppm, xpm, tiff, and ras, besides the common Web formats gif, jpeg, and xbm, which Navigator handles for you without your having to worry about it.

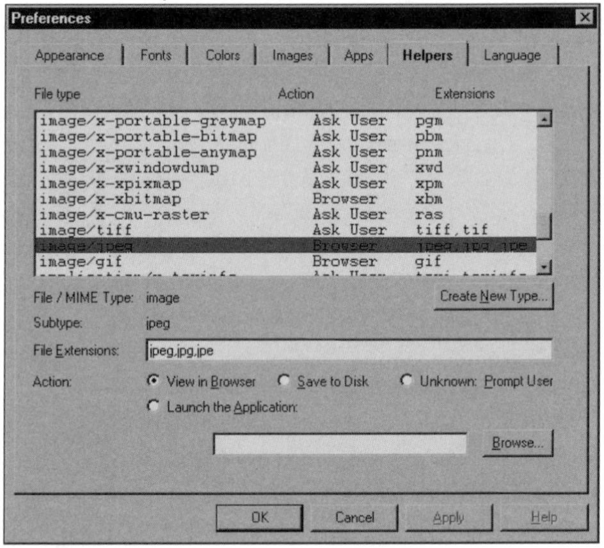

Those alphabet soup file extensions all refer to different ways of encoding a picture for storage as an ordinary computer data file. The granddaddy of them all is TIFF—the Tagged Image File Format, which can create humongous files. Many other formats, including the very popular GIF (Graphics Interchange Format), were invented in an attempt to compress the data more effectively. A few years ago, an expert committee called the Joint Photographic Experts Group thrashed out a new format which was supposed to supplant all others—hence, the JPEG (or .JPG) format.

Figure 6-1: *The Helpers panel contains 14 different image types. Yikes!*

The war between GIFs and JPEGs has been going on now for some time, and there is no clear winner, because, as it turns out, all images are not alike. For a simple image with just a few colors, GIFs often turn out to be both smaller in file size and offer better clarity. Hence, GIF is the format invariably used to create all the little "thumbnail" images that decorate Web pages. Because they are really considered part of the document (even though you can choose not to see them by unchecking Auto Load Images in the Options pull-down menu), they're known as "inline" images.

An "external" image is not part of the document you load, but it is referenced by a *link*—either hypertext, like an underlined word, or another type of link. These external images are frequently in JPEG format, to take advantage of the better color rendering that JPEG offers for more complex images. Where it gets confusing is when an inline GIF is used as the link to an external JPEG. It's actually a very common technique—it's used in the Matisse exhibit of the WebMuseum depicted in Figure 6-2.

For a complex picture, JPEG usually wins hands down on the file size contest, and usually delivers a higher quality image to boot. But because of the way the files are compressed, some images will lose something in clarity and color quality (it's often referred to as *lossy*). It was a great relief when most Web browsers began allowing both forms to be displayed inline, because then designers could choose the best format for a particular image.

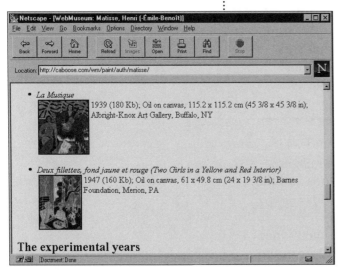

Figure 6-2: *These thumbnail images in GIF format lead to larger JPEG representations of the same painting that we can download.*

Now both formats are routinely used inline on Web pages. Netscape Navigator 2.0 has pushed this one step further by introducing the "progressive JPEG" to rival the "interlaced GIF." Both of these allow images to download in several successive passes, giving the user a more immediate scan of the image. Progressive JPEGs actually load marginally faster than plain JPEGs, and tend to look as though they're gradually improving their focus. Interlaced GIFs load marginally slower and look like a brick wall with smaller and smaller bricks.

 HOT TIP ___.___.___.___.___.___.___.___.___.__

For large images, you may want to enlarge your window. You can do this by getting rid of the Directory buttons, the Location window, and even the toolbar. In the Options pull-down menu, just uncheck the Show Toolbar, Show Location, and Show Directory buttons.

A less common image type encountered on Web pages, and which Netscape Navigator handles for you, is the bitmap or XBM image. These are two-color images used for simple line art or buttons and they are typically small in physical size—although a bitmap, being uncompressed, is not necessarily a small data file.

So what do you do about all those other image types we mentioned? Chances are, you won't need to worry about them at all. But if you've got specific requirements and need to access other image types, helper applications will come to the rescue.

Helper Applications for Images

There are, in fact, many other image types besides the ones in your Helpers panel that can be transferred over the Web, but because of the size of most images used in print media—where resolutions are much higher and file size is not as critical—they are not typically used on Web pages. But now that many other types of documents are being adapted for access over the Web, and Netscape Navigator has made it possible to view many of these file types, it is becoming more common to encounter some of these other image types.

Several helper applications are available for image viewing and manipulation, many of them available on the Net as shareware. Two of the more popular ones are LVIEWPro and Paint Shop Pro. More professional packages designed with desktop publishing capabilites are Adobe Photoshop, CorelDraw!, and Collage. The fancier the package, the more image types it handles. LVIEWPro, for instance, recognizes seven or eight image types, while Paint Shop Pro handles over thirty. Whether you need all this or not entirely depends on what you're using Netscape Navigator for. Companies who use Navigator for circulating in-house publications might have particular formats—say embedded pie charts in a PCX format—for which this could be useful.

To use any of these fancy image viewers, you need to tell Netscape Navigator that whenever it encounters an image of a particular type, it needs to launch another application to view it. Do this by specifying the image type and application in the Helpers preferences panel (see Chapter 5 for specifics.) If you prefer, you can save it to disk for viewing later: Switch the radio button between View in Browser and Save to Disk in the Helpers panel.

Actually, you might like to get and install the helper called LVIEWPro, and use it for images you especially prize even if they're in GIF and JPEG format. LVIEWPro lets you manipulate the image in ways Netscape Navigator's own viewer doesn't, so that you could, for example, resize an image or change the colors on a button to use it on your own home page. In Figure 6-3, we're resizing that Matisse JPEG we downloaded from the WebMuseum so we can add it to a little collection we're keeping for an art project.

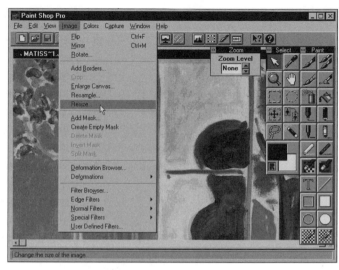

Figure 6-3: *We've downloaded that Matisse JPEG and now we're resizing it in Paint Shop Pro.*

 HOT TIP ━ ･ ━ ･ ━ ･ ━ ･ ━ ･ ━ ･ ━ ･

LVIEWPro is available at:
ftp://gatekeeper.dec.com/pub/micro/msdos/win3/desktop/

Paint Shop Pro, which handles many more image types and allows more sophisticated image manipulation, is available in a shareware trial version at:
ftp://isfs.kuis.kyoto-u.ac.jp/WINDOWS/graphic/PaintShopPro/

For fast skimming around the Web, many pros prefer to turn images off. You can do this by unchecking Auto Load Images under Options. Unfortunately, with the popularity of image maps on the Web (and the fact that many novice designers don't provide users a text alternative), that means that sometimes you get an empty page. You can reload the page with images by clicking the Image button. But you can also load one specific image and not others, by using the right mouse button and choosing the View This Image option.

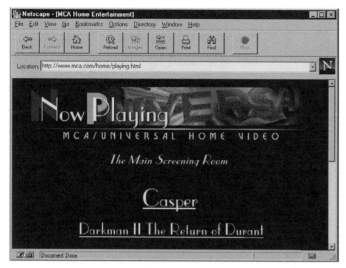

Figure 6-4: *Sit back and enjoy the show at your own computer if you have your video helper apps installed.*

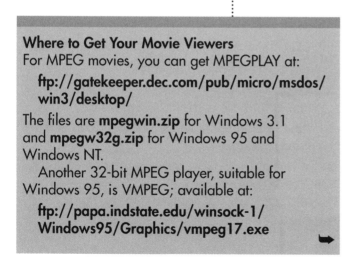

Where to Get Your Movie Viewers

For MPEG movies, you can get MPEGPLAY at:

> **ftp://gatekeeper.dec.com/pub/micro/msdos/win3/desktop/**

The files are **mpegwin.zip** for Windows 3.1 and **mpegw32g.zip** for Windows 95 and Windows NT.

Another 32-bit MPEG player, suitable for Windows 95, is VMPEG; available at:

> **ftp://papa.indstate.edu/winsock-1/Windows95/Graphics/vmpeg17.exe**

QuickTime & MPEG Movies

Movies on the Web, fortunately, do not come in such a bewildering variety of formats and flavors. Most of them are either in the Macintosh standard known as QuickTime, or are the product of another expert committee, the Motion Picture Experts Group—guess what? An MPEG, of course. They are about equally common, and the allegiance of Mac and Windows to the two rival formats is now pretty much irrelevant. A third standard, Microsoft's AVI format, has also begun to elbow in on the action lately.

Netscape Navigator has no built-in movie viewer, so you really need helpers if you want to view movies on the Web. If you're equipped with movie helpers, you can enjoy Web services like Universal's new sneak previews (Figure 6-4). Better have plenty of disk space, though: these short clips are around 2MB each!

Therein lies the problem with movies on the Web at this point in time as we approach the end of the 20th century and get set to see what the 21st will bring. The professional video you see on your TV every day is delivered to you at 30 frames per second in a screen resolution quality that allows it to be viewed on screen sizes from miniature to wall-size. But the amount of information that video represents in digital form is about 30MB per second. The Web, and your little home computer, are not capable of that.

The solution to this problem is data compression. Each of the three current standards goes about this compression differently. But no matter how you do it, something gets lost along the way. Most of the movie files you will download off the Web will only play relatively smoothly in a small thumbnail-size screen. The frames you see in Figure 6-5 are shown in their actual size as they played on our screen with QuickTime. If you enlarge the screen size to take up your entire computer screen, you'll find the movie "skipping" frames in order to try to keep up with the sound, and the resolution of the picture frame looking somewhat abstract. Try this when you've installed your movie player—it's got its own interesting charm, but it's obviously not movie theater quality.

Like many things in the computer field these days, video is one that will undoubtedly be making big strides in the next few years. If you want to keep up with it as it grows, get your movie viewers and keep checking in on those interesting and growing movie sites every few months.

Install your movie viewer the same as your audio player, if you want it to launch automatically when you encounter a movie file. Actually, though, we recommend that you set your helper application to Save rather than Launch Application because down-loading a movie file takes a while. If you save it first, you'll be able to replay it, and if there's a playback problem, at least you won't have to go through the download again. Don't forget that anytime you like you can use the right mouse button and choose the Save As option to save a movie or audio file, the same as you would a text file.

Figure 6-5: *Musician/artist Deborah Harry in a frame from a movie clip advertising a live Web concert, shown actual size in our Quicktime movie player.*

QuickTime 2.0.3 for Windows is available at:
http://quicktime.apple.com

To play AVI movies, you can get Video for Windows (the file is **avivie42.zip**) from:

ftp://gatekeeper.dec.com/pub/micro/msdos/ win3/desktop/

A runtime version of MS Video for Windows is available as **vfw11a.exe** from:

ftp.microsoft.com/developr/drg/multimedia/

Audio

The surprising thing about Web audio files, at least to those of us who are non-experts, is that often they can rival video files in size. It's not uncommon to find a conventional sound file lasting just 30 seconds taking up several megabytes of disk space.

A really well-behaved Web page tells you how big an audio or video file is, so you can decide whether you have that much time to spend downloading it. Unfortunately, many HTML authors get too carried away by their artistic page makeup to worry about "technical details" like that (or are working on university supercomputers and don't think about those of us on little PCs), and the information is not available. Netscape Navigator helps things along—it will generally give you progress information at the lower left corner of the screen. So if you're already running late for an appointment and you see "8% of 456K" down there, that's when you click on Stop to bail out.

It's nice of whatever courtier was delegated to make the "First Family" page from The White House (Figure 6-6) to tell us that the sound of Socks mewing is a 36K file. They were also nice enough to provide us with a choice of .AU or .WAV files—or even a text file (must have been some lobby group behind that).

Sound Power (Windows 3.1)   Here's how to make your tinny little PC loudspeaker work for a living. If you can't afford a SoundBlaster (or don't want to make your system *too* attractive to the kids), you can divert audio to your built-in PC speaker—the one that thought it was going to spend its entire life saying nothing more elaborate than "BEEP." Follow these steps:

1. Grab WPLANY.EXE from the FTP site and install it.

2. Go to the Options/General-Helper Apps panel and instruct Netscape Navigator to launch WPLANY whenever you download .WAV, .AU, or .SND files.

3. Grab a file called SPEAK.EXE from **ftp:// ftp.cam.org/systems/ms-windows/slip-ppp/ viewers/** or **ftp://ftp.microsoft.com/Softlib/ MSLFILES/**.

4. Put SPEAK.EXE in its own directory and run it under DOS. It will self-extract, producing the files SPEAKER.DRV and OEMSETUP.INF.

5. Fire up Windows, and activate the Control Panel utility (in the Main program group).

6. Click on Drivers, then select the Add button. Select Unlisted Or Updated Driver from the list. Enter the path to the OEMSETUP.INF you just created (that's what Windows is looking for).   ➡

Audio files come in many different formats, and the trade-off is basically the same as for images—quality vs. file size. The main sound file types you're likely to come across are .AU, .AIF, .SND, and .WAV. The .AU file format is typically used when file size is at a premium and high fidelity is not important. It's good for voices (like Socks's mewing) but no great shakes for music. .AIF and .WAV files typically have higher sample rates and produce higher fidelity, which makes them much better for music.

Our advice is the same as for movie files: Set your Helper Applications to Save rather than Launch your application immediately. We'll add more advice, too: Don't let these things accumulate on your hard drive—they're just too big to give house-room to unless you have good reason.

Netscape Navigator for Windows has its own audio player, NAPlayer which plays .AU, .AIF, and .SND audio files. You'll see the NAPLAYER.EXE file in the Navigator directory, but be aware that in order for it to work, you still need a sound card. By default, Navigator sets the Helpers list to launch NAPlayer when it sees an .AU, .AIF, or .SND audio file type. Unless you change that for your own favorite audio player, it will automatically launch the program when you click on an active link to an audio file.

Once the file is open, you can control the playing of the file by using the control buttons on the NAPlayer toolbar (see Figure 6-6). If you set your

7. If all is well, "Sound Driver for PC-Speaker" will pop up as the single item on a list. Select OK. You'll hear otherworldly sounds as your little speaker wakes up and says, "Oh wow! I get to do something more important than BEEP?"

8. Choose Restart Windows.

9. Now you'll hear things whenever you end a Windows session or select an illegal option. If this does not please you, bring back the Control Panel, click on Sounds, and uncheck the Enable System Sounds box. ➡

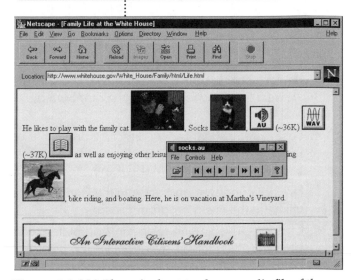

Figure 6-6: *NA Player is about to play an audio file of the First Feline mewing.*

10. Any audio you grab from the Net is going to sound really terrible. Quit being so stingy—go out and buy a sound card. The computer hardware industry needs your money!

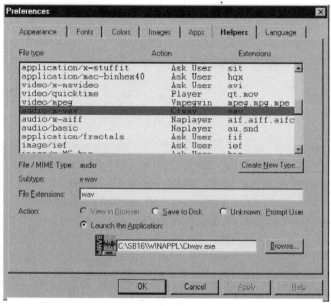

Figure 6-7: *We're putting SoundBlaster in charge of playing those neat music files we hope to come across here.*

Helpers panel to Save to Disk for audio files, you can play the files yourself once they've downloaded by starting up NAPlayer. You have to install the NAPlayer icon in a Windows program group - yourself—Netscape Navigator does not automatically do this for you.

Most music lovers will want to have another sound player available for playing .WAV files, since they're the most common type on the Web for music files. If you have SoundBlaster, you can set your SoundBlaster player as a helper. Find the file **ctwav.exe** in your SoundBlaster directory and designate that in the line for files with the wav extension in the Helpers panel. (See Figure 6-7.)

One of the best audio players available by FTP is called WPLANY, short for "We Play Anything." The file is **wplny09b.zip** and you can find it at: **ftp://ftp.cam.org/systems/ms-windows/slip-ppp/viewers/**

Another audio player—highly sophisticated—is WHAM, which is available at the same site as WPLANY under the name **wham1310.zip**.

Of course, to hear any of these wild and wonderful sounds you need a sound card and a pair of loudspeakers. Or do you? For a cheap solution, see the "Sound Power" sidebar beginning on page 123.

Real-time Audio & Video

One of the more exciting developments in audio on the Web recently has been the advent of "real-time" audio and video, or more accurately audio and video on demand. What this means is that instead of sitting and drumming your fingers waiting for that humongous audio file to download and begin playing, you can click on an audio and/or video link and begin playing almost immediately, as soon as the first few packets of information arrive. As the information "streams" in, the play continues with no interruption (although this may depend a great deal on your setup).

While video still has some major hurdles to overcome, real-time audio is well on the road to being ready for the average computer user's consumption. By some miracle of new compression technology, the files are also actually a lot smaller than conventional sound files. A file for RealAudio, one of the early leaders in the field, is about 1KB per second of playing time, which means an entire hour's recording fits in about 3.6MB, and you don't even have to download it all at once. You can log onto the Web in the morning, check into the National Public Radio site, click on "Morning Edition," and listen to the morning program stream in as you have your coffee and answer your e-mail. Lately some trial efforts have even been posted for "live" sports broadcasts.

The RealAudio Player is available on the Web at http://www.realaudio.com.

Some RealAudio & Internet Wave Sites

RealAudio has made such great strides in the last year that now many major broadcasting outfits host RealAudio Web pages where you can hear the latest news broadcasts or listen to the daily entertainment shows whenever you want. Some of the best real-time audio sites online now are:

ABC Radio News:
http://www.abcradionet.com

National Public Radio:
http://www.realaudio.com/contentp/npr.html

Canadian Broadcasting Company:
http://www.radio.cbc.ca/

Bootcamp: A Report on Computers and Technology (heard on CBS Radio):
http://www.pulver.com:80/bootcamp/

Internet Radio Hawaii:
http://www.hotspots.hawaii.com/

I-Rock Radio:
http://www.iRock.Com/

For the latest additions to the RealAudio and Internet Wave sites, go to the RealAudio home page at **http://www.realaudio.com/** and the I-Wave home page at **http://vocaltec.com/iwave.htm**.

Virtual Worlds with WebFX   Visit some wild and wooly places with the new VRML (Virtual Reality Modeling Language) viewer by Paper Software. WebFX is designed to be an instant plug-in to Netscape Navigator, making a seamless interface with your browser. The list of virtual reality sites is growing daily. The place to keep up with all this is at the Paper Software Web site (see address below).

WebFX requires at least a 486DX/33MHZ computer with 8MB RAM, and a 256 color display. If you have a 486SX or a 486 notebook, you must have a math coprocessor.

Get information about WebFX and virtual reality sites at: **http://www.paperinc.com/**.

This is still developing technology, so the sound quality can be somewhat variable and is very dependent on the audio setup in your own computer. It has been likened at its best to AM Radio, and that's a fair analogy. It's best for voice broadcasts and lacks the range for really fine-quality music recordings.

Another up and coming real-time audio contender (with slightly better sound quality) is Internet Wave. Again, the quality of the sound you receive is dependent on your audio card and general computer setup. As of this writing, the Internet Wave player is available in a beta version at **http://www.vocaltec.com/iwave.htm**.

If you get turned on by real-time audio, you can also get encoders for each of these systems and convert your own sound files or recordings into RealAudio or Internet Wave format.

Note: In order for real-time audio to work as advertised, the host computer where the real-time audio files are kept must also have a RealAudio or Internet Wave server. If not, the files will download in the usual way, and the player will be launched after the download is complete. But even if you can't play it in "real time," this can be very useful for long-playing audio files very quickly, since the file size is considerably smaller and downloads much quicker.

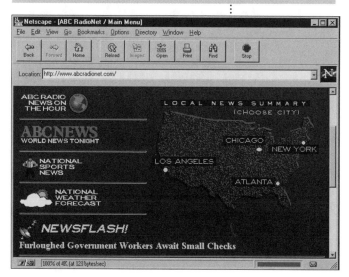

Figure 6-8: *Get news online 24 hours a day, 7 days a week with RealAudio.*

Other Helper Applications

As the World Wide Web grows in popularity, many people are discovering ways to use it to exchange different kinds of documents rather than just HTML files. It's possible to transfer and view documents of other types with Netscape using special viewers as attachments. All you need to do is define them in your Helpers preferences panel. A few of the more popular ones you might be able to use are described here.

Acrobat Amber Reader

Publications designed for print are usually designed in formats such as Rich Text or PostScript. These contain complicated layouts and formatting that are either not possible to simulate in HTML, or doing so would present far too big a project. However, having access to things like journals, archived issues of magazines, and detailed government documents can be a valuable research tool.

Adobe has produced software that allows such documents to be converted into a "Portable Document Format" (.pdf) which then allows them to be distributed over the Web, as well as through e-mail and over corporate networks. While the conversion software is a commercial package, the Acrobat Amber Reader is free.

If you have the Acrobat Amber Reader, you can install it as a helper application with Netscape Navigator and use it to download and read .pdf files posted on the Web. Some of the .pdf files available include an online version of *The New York Times* (see Figure 6-9), a number of journals and books, tax forms from the IRS, and various government documents.

Moving frame shows the portion of the page currently on display.

Figure 6-9: *You can read the online version of* The New York Times *with Acrobat Amber Reader.*

You can get information about the the Acrobat Reader and download it at: **http://www.adobe.com/Software/Acrobat/**.

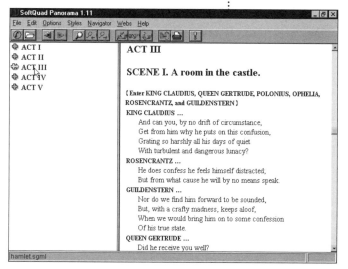

Figure 6-10: *The complete works of Shakespeare in annotated form are available as an SGML document that you can read with Panorama as a helper app.*

Panorama & SGML

HTML is actually a subset of an older Internet standard for exchanging documents: Standard Generalized Markup Language, or SGML. SGML is particularly suited to highly annotated documents, such as dictionaries, technical documentation, catalogs, government publications, academic journals, and newspapers.

Many SGML documents coexist peacefully on the Web with HTML, but in order to appreciate their full referencing capabilities you need to have an SGML reader. Panorama is an SGML browser produced by SoftQuad which you can use as a stand-alone SGML browser or install as a helper application to Netscape Navigator.

You can get more information about SGML on the Web at: **http://www.ncsa.uiuc.edu/SDG/Software/Mosaic/WebSGML.html**.

And you can get a free version of Panorama at: **http://www.oclc.org:5046/oclc/research/panorama/panorama.html**.

About Java

The hot word on the Web circuits these days is something called *Java*, which was developed by Sun Microsystems. Many developers are convinced that Java will transform the Web from static presentation of two-dimensional pages to a truly interactive hypermedia.

What Java does is make it possible to run small programs called "applets" within Netscape Navigator to produce active events. For example, a logo can be made to revolve or change, small animations can play in a part of the screen, an audio file can be programmed to play when you access a page, or a game can be made to respond to user input.

So what do you need to do to take advantage of this? Nothing. Java has been incorporated into Netscape Navigator 2.0, so you should already be able to access pages with Java applets and see it in action. The best way to gain an understanding of Java is to access some Java-enabled Web pages and see for yourself. A good reference for current Java demo pages is the Java site at Sun Microsystems: **http://www.javasoft.com/applets/applets.html**. For more examples, check **http://www.gamelan.com**.

The only thing you should be aware of is that, like real-time audio and video, Java is still developing on the Web. As designers and programmers put their heads together on this, we're apt to see a whole explosion of interesting Java applications. But don't be too distressed if an occasional Java page doesn't work as advertised or crashes your browser. Just stay tuned and watch it grow. And look for Netscape updates that will be even more Java-friendly.

Internet Services via Netscape Navigator

After a few weeks of cruising the Web, you get so used to seeing **http://** up there in the URL window that you might start thinking of the entire Internet world in terms of http addresses. In fact, http (HyperText Transport Protocol) is the data-exchange protocol that made the Web possible, but it's far from being the only allowable prefix to URL addresses. Actually, it merely specifies a type of server—the one whose exact address makes up the next part of the URL.

Almost all the "traditional" Internet protocols have server addresses that are accessible by Netscape Navigator. It's perfectly legitimate to construct a URL beginning **gopher://**, **ftp://**, or **telnet://**, and by a kind of trickery, the prefix **mailto:** brings e-mail transmission to your Navigator screen. Even Finger (get login information) and Archie (search FTP sites for keywords) services are available, thanks to so-called "gateways" made available by some major Web servers and accessed as http addresses.

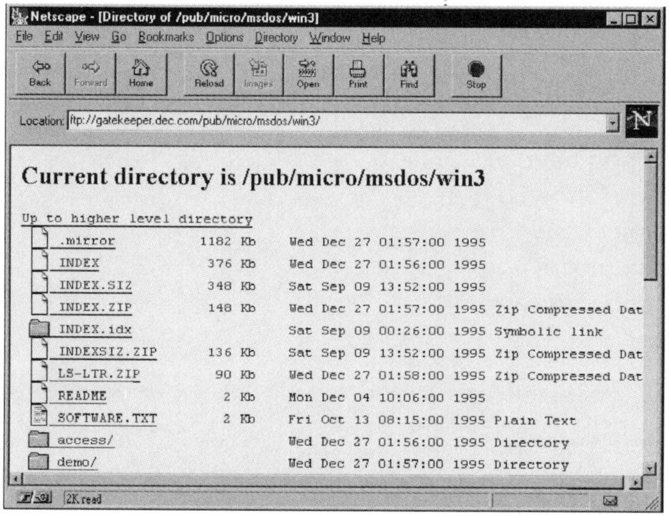

Figure 6-11: *A popular FTP archive for Windows desktop applications is the gatekeeper.dec.com site shown here.*

FTP

Both of us are old enough net-jockeys to remember when anonymous FTP (File Transfer Protocol) was a real chore. There was a lot to type—with perfect accuracy—just to get connected. Directory listings would whiz by out of control; you'd have to remember to switch between ASCII and binary modes to get your downloads right; to inspect a README file, you'd have to pipe it through a separate UNIX pager; and in general the command set was about what you'd expect for one of the oldest forms of Internetting there is.

The first move in the direction of user-friendliness was the invention of the UNIX program **ncftp**, which at least logged on for you, remembered your favorite sites and directories, and provided a way of displaying all those README files. Today, Windows-based FTP applications easily handle automatic login, scrolling of directory listings, and README by mouse (as seen in Figure 2-4 in Chapter 2).

Netscape Navigator has one of the best FTP programs there is, incorporated right within the browser—it does all that, plus displays directory listings with an icon accompanying each entry showing what type of file it is (see Figure 6-11). When it comes to a download, you don't have to decide whether this is supposed to be binary or ASCII: Navigator already knows. When you click on a file icon, Navigator follows whatever instructions you have given it on how to handle file types in your Helpers preferences panel. Or it prompts you by telling you, "No viewer configured for this application. How would you like to handle it?" Just choose Save to Disk and tell it where you want to put it.

To send a file to a remote FTP site, first access the site. If you have a login username and password enter the login username first followed by an @ sign, then enter the host, as in the following example: **ftp:// username@www.thegroup.net**. You will be prompted for your password. Choose Upload File from the File pulldown menu, and you can then browse your directories for the file you wish to send.

𝛀 HOT TIP

Keep a list of your often-visited FTP sites in a special bookmark subdirectory. Their URL addresses all begin "ftp://..." and ftp often appears twice in the complete address—for example, **ftp://ftp.digital.com.**

Gopher

The Internet Gopher was always a much friendlier way of accessing what's out there: It actually reads many of the same data sources that FTP, Telnet, and WAIS do, but it strips out the jargon and reduces everything to a menu choice. You can start anywhere and get anywhere from any starting point in the great labyrinth of Gopher-burrows. One good starting point is the "Gopher Jewels" menu maintained by the University of Southern California. Its URL is **gopher://cwis.usc.edu:70/ 11/Other_Gophers_and_Information_Resources/Gopher-Jewels**.

One difficulty we always had, when searching for something with the Gopher, was remembering which Gopher-burrows we had already explored. Netscape Navigator's color change for "followed links" applies as much to Gopher menu items as it does to Web pages, and it's a terrific help. So is the Back button.

In a sense, the philosophy of the Gopher, invented at the University of Minnesota, laid the groundwork for the World Wide Web by showing that Internet resources could be made accessible to the kind of people who did not care to learn FTP commands and never found out the difference between a binary and an ASCII file transfer. Soon the Gopher may be a victim of the phenomenal success of the Web. One Gopher site we've used more times than we could count has just announced that it is going "out of business" in favor of a super-duper Web page.

Telnet

Like Gopher, many of the services offered by Telnet are being revised these days into a more accessible Web format. The Telnet protocol is the one you use to connect your computer directly to another computer, which may be in Australia as easily as in Washington, DC. Your computer then acts as if it were a terminal on the host computer allowing you to execute programs and read files, but not download.

We used to Telnet often to the library of Dartmouth College (**baker.dartmouth.edu**) to use their searchable Shakespeare to help with the cryptic crosswords we're addicted to. Now that we've discovered the hypertext Shakespeare (**http://the-tech.mit.edu/Shakespeare/ works.html**), we won't be going to Dartmouth so often. However, Telnet is far from obsolete—if you ever need to do any serious database searching, you're going to get to know Telnet and the WAIS services (Wide Area Information Services) Telnet can get you to.

Netscape Navigator needs helper software to complete a Telnet connection. One we use is QVTNET—a 32-bit Windows application obtainable from **ftp://ftp.iastate.edu/pub/pc/win3**. There are also others. Whatever you choose, tell Navigator about it in the Apps preferences panel of General Preferences.

Archie

Archie is the Internet service that allows you to search every FTP site in the world for directory and file names containing a keyword that you're interested in— "beatle," let's say. Even though there's no such thing as a URL beginning "archie://...," this wonderful service is available on the Web thanks to so-called hypertext "gateways" provided at several Web sites.

Go to **http://hoohoo.ncsa.uiuc.edu/archie.html** and you'll find all the Archie commands wrapped up in one fill-out-and-submit Web page. (See Figures 6-12 and 6-13).

First you'll see a box for you to enter your keyword(s). Then comes a pop-up menu of four different search types; the default is not case-sensitive and it searches for the string, not the word (which means that *Beatles* would be found by searching for *beatle*). Radio buttons allow you to choose between a sort By Host computer or By Date. Another pop-up menu allows you to choose the "niceness" rating of your search—Not Nice at All/Nice/ Nicer/Very Nice/Extremely Nice/Nicest. Archie servers are in demand, and there's always a queue of users wait-

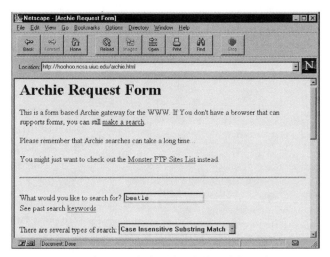

Figure 6-12: *This search for "beatle" took less than a minute and produced 33 files to choose from.*

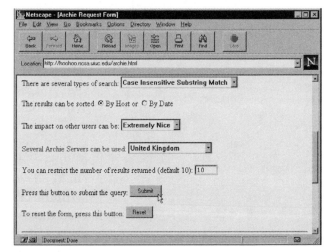

Figure 6-13: *Some of the options on the Archie request form at NCSA.*

ing for search results. Niceness is basically a way of saying "After you—I insist" or "Do you mind?—I'm in a real hurry." If you accept the default "Very Nice," you will barge ahead of somebody who has rated her search "Nicest." (We're looking forward to the day when this menu comes up changed to Polite/Cool/Supercilious/Bloody Rude.) If you're not in a hurry and can do something else in the meantime, you might consider being Extremely Nice.

One more pop-up menu is a selection of Archie servers. Pick one that's geographically close. Finally, you may also have options to restrict the search by the domain and number of hits. All this to save you from having to compose a UNIX command like: **archie -s -m100 -N5000 beatle**.

Searches can take a while—the nicer, the longer, obviously—but Netscape Navigator makes life very easy once the results are in. The hit list becomes a hypertext document which you can scroll, save, or click on to go straight to the likeliest source of that Beatles lyric you were looking for. Truly luxurious search-and-grab.

Finger

The Department of Computer Science of the University of Indiana has kindly provided another hypertext gateway—this one to Finger services. Its address is **http://www.cs.indiana.edu/finger/**.

Finger was originally used in UNIX networks to find out who else was logged on, to see when they last checked their e-mail, and to consult project files created for that specific purpose. "Project files" has come to mean all sorts of weird things. Add **dmc.iris.washington.edu/spyder** onto Finger's address, and you'll get a readout of recent seismic events worldwide. California residents can get information about their Congressional representatives by fingering **sen.ca.gov/** followed by their zip code. And then there's always the state of the Coca Cola machine at various U.S. universities. Carnegie-Mellon (**coke.elab.cs.cmu.edu**) was the first to make their Coke fingerable, and others have followed. There may also be baseball scores, weather forecasts, and Nielsen ratings out there in Finger-space—the sites change too frequently for a book to be a very reliable source of good Finger addresses.

In general, a user@host address needs to be formatted as host/user for the Indiana gateway. So to find out about someone whose e-mail address is **ualee@mcl.ucsb.edu**, you have to type: **http:// www.cs.indiana.edu/finger/mcl.ucsb.edu/ualee**.

If you don't specify a user, you're likely to get a readout of everyone logged in to that host machine.

The actual source of the information Finger conveys is the first line of a file called ".project," and the whole of a file called ".plan" (these conventions originated at UC Berkeley). One or both have to be present in the user's home directory. An example is shown in Figure 6-14. If you want to provide some information of interest to somebody who Fingers you, you need to have a UNIX shell account and simply make up those files.

Forms & Security

There are many times when it's appropriate for the flow of information from the Web to be put in reverse: when you need to put information "in" rather than pull it "out." One simple case in point is searching for keywords—how's a Web searcher to know what *you* want to know if you can't tell it?

Another simple example is a feedback page, on which somebody invites you to enter some informa-

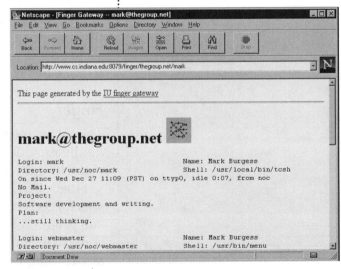

Figure 6-14: *We're checking to see what our sysadmin is up to right now.*

tion. Netscape invites your feedback in a page you'll find under "How to Give Feedback" in the main menu's Help pull-down menu. All such page features are known collectively as "forms," and they seem to get more complex and more ingenious all the time.

Undoubtedly, one of the driving forces behind the development of forms is Web commerce. More and more entrepreneurs are jumping onto the Web these days, attempting to sell everything from t-shirts and protein bars to flowers and airline tickets. But in order for these commercial ventures to really take off, everyone is aware that some method of security is necessary to ensure that any personal or financial information you send over the Web is not intercepted and put to devious use by villains.

For ordinary transactions like searching keywords and providing feedback to page authors, this may not concern you. But entering and sending credit card information over the Net should rightly give you reason for pause. And if you're contemplating anything like online banking, you'll certainly want to be sure the transactions are secure.

Netscape provides several levels of security for users. The most secure transactions are those conducted over "secure servers." This means that when you connect to a secure site, the host machine does a security "handshake" during which Netscape and the server agree on the security code they will use. From then on, transactions between the two are encrypted. The encryption method that Netscape uses (40-bit RC4) means that, on average, a 64-MIPS (million instructions per second) computer would need a year of dedicated processor time to break the message's encryption. So you can feel fairly confident that information you send through a secure page is protected. But, of course, the ultimate decision is yours.

You can tell if you have connected to a secure server when the security colorbar appears on the top of your screen and the broken key in the bottom left corner becomes whole. You can also check the Document Information in the View menu for security information. Also, when you enter or leave a secure space, various informative dialog boxes will be displayed. Figure 6-15 shows the warning we got when attempting to order t-shirts with a credit card on one Web site.

Perhaps you're the sort of person who doesn't care about security. Or you care about it enough that your policy is never to send personal or financial information over the Net. In either case, if you don't want to be bothered with these security messages, you can disable the display of these security messages in the Security Preferences panel under the Options menu.

Moving On

By now you should be aware that the Web is all things to all people. Perhaps you're still just enjoying exploring, or maybe you've found your own little niche of favorite sites run by like-minded Web users. Maybe you're feeling like you'd like to stake your claim on a little patch in this frontier.

In the next chapter, we'll show you how to do that. We'll tell you a bit about Web page design and start you off on designing a simple page in HTML. Your imagination and ambition can take off from there.

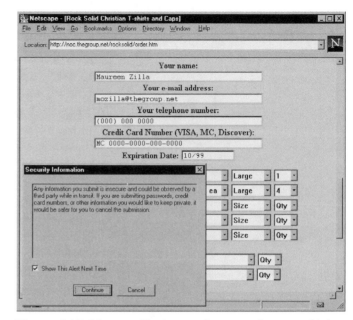

Figure 6-15: *Netscape Navigator gives us a chance to think again before sending our credit card information to this t-shirt vendor on the Web.*

MAKING YOUR OWN WEB DOCUMENTS

In Chapter 5 you saw how Netscape Navigator actually creates a personal Web page for you with the Bookmark menu. It only takes a little imagination to wonder whether you couldn't personalize it a little—say, insert your own picture and some info you'd like to include about yourself—and save it as a home page file.

We'll show you how in this chapter. So that you understand all the basics of HTML composition, we'll start fresh and design a complete Web page with inline images and hypertext links. You'll be able to copy any of our techniques for yourself—and we'll give you detailed instructions on how to exploit the New Age of Plagiarism.

HTML: The Language of the Web

Go to a Web page—any old page will do—and pick the menu choice View/by Document Source. What you see is HTML. Look scary?

Awww, c'mon—it's not like a real computer language. At least you can see some ordinary English text in there (okay, if you picked a Spanish site you can see Spanish).

Mixed in with the text, sometimes quite densely, are a lot of things like <H1>, </H1>, <P>, </P>, <A HREF="file">, and so on. Those are just the tags that the Web browser needs to interpret the author's page. They often occur in pairs such as <H1> for a start tag, </H1> for an end tag. Some HTML authors use lowercase letters—some use a mixture of uppercase and lowercase. Frankly, my dear, the Web doesn't give a damn.

An entire HTML document is (usually) enclosed within a tag pair, like this:

```
<HTML> ...everything in the document
</HTML>
```

It needs to be subdivided once only, like this:

```
<HTML>
<HEAD>
...everything in the header: Title, document type, etc.
</HEAD>
<BODY>
...everything in the body (in other words, everything that's actually
going to appear on the page).
</BODY>
</HTML>
```

Starting with that simple framework, which you can see in Figure 7-1, we're going to build a home page for you visually, explaining each new element as we add it.

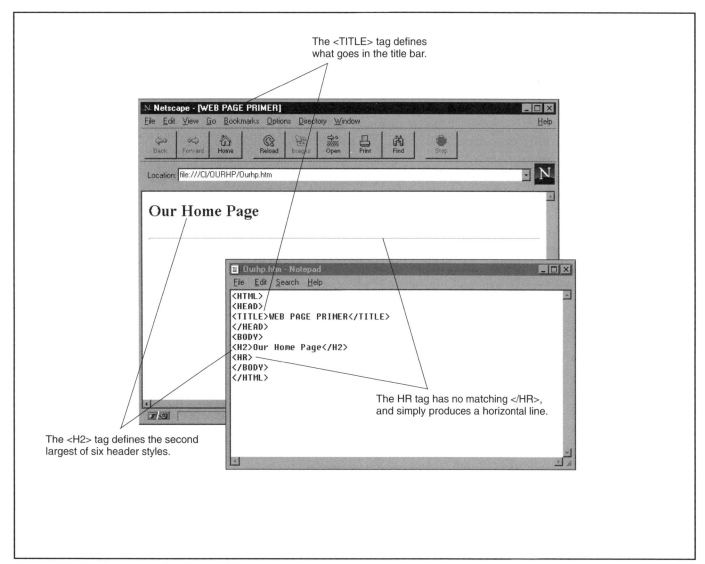

The <TITLE> tag defines what goes in the title bar.

The HR tag has no matching </HR>, and simply produces a horizontal line.

The <H2> tag defines the second largest of six header styles.

Figure 7-1: *Making a start: Header and HR tags.*

Building a Home Page

The way we normally work is to have our HTML text file in Notepad (or any text editor) in the left two-thirds of the screen, and Netscape Navigator up (but not connected to the Net) in the right two-thirds of the screen. They overlap but can be brought into the foreground just by clicking. The local file is loaded into Navigator initially by the menu choice File/Open File, or by pressing Ctrl-O. We use the Reload toolbar button or Ctrl-R thereafter. After each change we make to the HTML file, we save the file and reload the page into Navigator to see what effect our change has had. We always use the file extension .htm or .html (see the sidebar), although Navigator does not check files at the door and turn away any that aren't named correctly.

All of the text we want to put in our Web page is defined first as paragraphs. Every paragraph begins with <P> and ends with </P>. The end tag for a paragraph is optional, but it helps to keep the sections of text clear. HTML ignores all line breaks and carriage returns in a source file (they're interpreted simply as a space), and only creates a paragraph break when it sees </P> or a new <P>. In Figure 7-2, you can see how all of the basic text in our page is set up in eight paragraphs.

Next we'd like to make a proper list out of our travel diary entries. We'll choose the <OL> tag, for an Ordered List. We could have picked <UL>Unordered list, or <DL>Definition List. We replace the <P> at the beginning of our list text with <OL> and the </P> at the end with </OL>. Then we encase each element in the list within the <LI>...</LI> codes (for List Item). Like the </P> tag, </LI> is optional,

HTM or HTML? Some Web documents have the extension .htm and others .html. Why is that? Well, .html is the logical full extension for HTML files, as used by most of the Web gurus who work on UNIX and Sun stations around the world, as well as Apple computers. Those of us working in the DOS universe of PCs were until recently restricted to the DOS rules of eight-letter file names with three letter extensions. Thus, the shorthand .htm version. Windows 95 changed all this by allowing long filenames. But it's the server computer on which you post your files that will dictate what extension you should use, either .htm or .html. You should check with your Web service provider for their requirements.

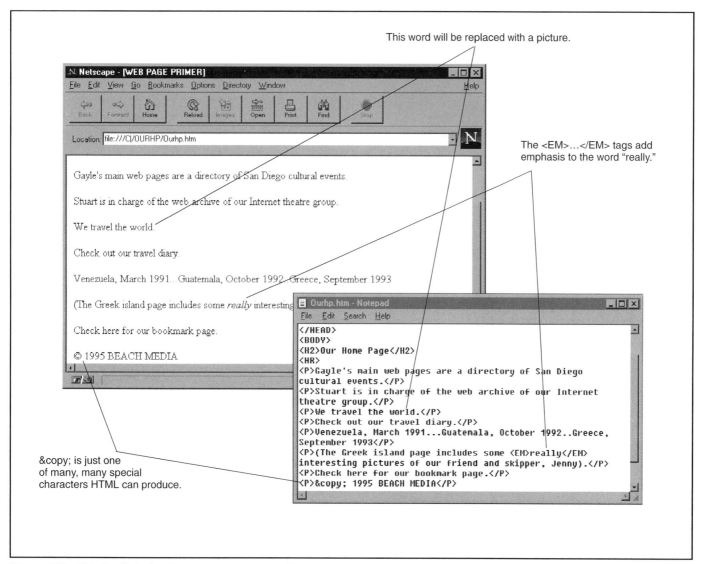

This word will be replaced with a picture.

The <EM>...</EM> tags add emphasis to the word "really."

© is just one of many, many special characters HTML can produce.

Figure 7-2: *This is all the basic text we want to put in.*

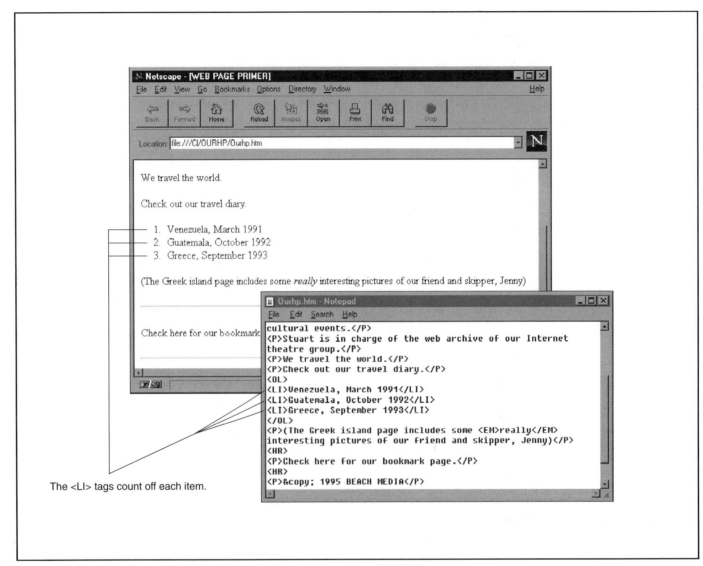

The <LI> tags count off each item.

Figure 7-3: *Making a proper list.*

since it will be assumed by the next <LI>, but we're going to include it here to keep things clear. We don't need to add the numbers—Netscape Navigator will do that. The results are shown in Figure 7-3.

Adding Images & Links

As discussed in Chapter 6, by far the safest format for inline "thumbnail" images is the .GIF format. For larger pictures you can also use .JPG. Netscape Navigator allows .XBM and .XPM, as well, but all graphical browsers support .GIF and most, but not all, now support .JPG. If you don't have your own scanner to scan in your favorite holiday snapshots, you'll need to find either a friend with a scanner (such people are getting more and more popular) or a lab or service bureau that can do it. There are a lot of technical terms involved in scanning, but your requirement is simple and straightforward: you need a color .GIF or .JPG no wider than 600 pixels (the full width of the Navigator window on an ordinary PC). The data file should not be over, say, 75K—and it should reduce a lot when you crop it and size it. Anything bigger has more definition than anybody will ever see and will simply make the page slow to load. One service we've used charges $9.95 and they shoot in 24 hours—or faster for more money. Your local copy shop may even be able to do this for you.

You're going to need some image management software (LVIEWPro works fine for this) to allow you to do your own cropping and sizing. Contrast adjustments and various enhancement techniques are both worth attempting once you gain a little confidence. You can play all kinds of fancy games keeping icon libraries and inline directories, but for the sake of simplicity let's assume the complete kit—the HTML file plus all hypermedia files—is in the Netscape directory.

So, once you've got the .GIFs all cropped, sized, and assembled, you call each of them into your page with the tag **<IMG SRC="filename.GIF">**. You can see the results in Figure 7-4.

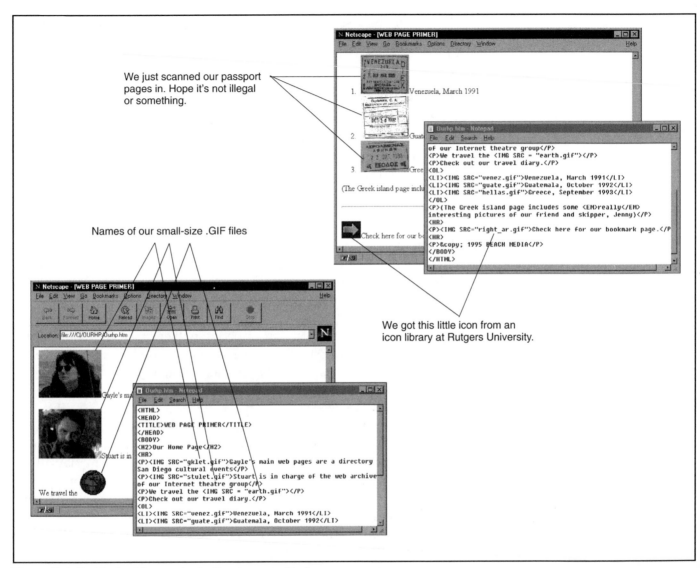

We just scanned our passport pages in. Hope it's not illegal or something.

Names of our small-size .GIF files

We got this little icon from an icon library at Rutgers University.

Figure 7-4: *Suddenly this page is starting to come alive!*

That's already nice, but a couple of adjustments to the "World" in-line are in order. First, it would be nice if the middle of the image lines up with the text rather than the bottom. Second, if we intend to post our page on the Web, we have to bear in mind that not everyone is seeing this page in a graphical Web browser. There are perfectly good—and very fast—text browsers. Lynx is the most popular.

Lynx users, if we don't help them out, will see that line as:

We travel the [IMAGE]

The way to help them out is to make use of ALT, meaning "If you can't show an image, here's what to replace it with." If you're making your page just for your own use, of course, you needn't bother. Both of those fixups are shown in Figure 7-5.

Links

Well, this is supposed to be hypertext, right? It's time we "hypered" off to some other destinations.

A hypertext link (we'll just call it a link from now on) is signaled by two elements combined. The first is an anchor in the form <A> ...something... </A>, where the something is the word or picture that the user will click on to activate the link. The second is a reference in the form HREF="...something..." and in this case the something is where the link leads to—a different part of this document, another document, an external image or other hypermedia file, or a URL address on a completely different computer possibly in a different country.

One document we're definitely going to need to link to is our travel diary, which is a separate document in our own computer called "trdiary.htm." To turn the word "Venezuela" into a link to its part of "trdiary.htm" we write the combined tags like this:

<A HREF="trdiary.htm#Lagunetas">Venezuela</A>

This fixes the image alignment.

This fixes things for Lynx users.

Figure 7-5: *Fixing a couple of little problems.*

That "#Lagunetas" tagged on to the file name tells Netscape Navigator to go to the internal label "Lagunetas" which is buried somewhere in "trdiary.htm." The matching tag in that file is <A NAME="Lagunetas">, which should be followed by </A>, but doesn't need to enclose anything.

Now, if we take a look at the top half of the page, we'll see that the inline .GIFs themselves can be made into links. It's just a matter of wrapping the anchor codes around everything correctly, like so: <A HREF="filename"><IMG SRC="filename"></A>.

Note that the full-size "external" pictures (see Figure 7-7) can be any format, and many are in regular use on the Web. It explains why Netscape Navigator's Helpers preferences panel is so complicated.

That Extra Netscape Pizzazz

HTML was always thought of as a way of describing the format of document *content*, and specifically *not* the actual design of the page. All questions of layout and appearance are supposed to be left to the user—hence all the options Netscape Navigator (and other browsers) allow in the Preferences panels for you to choose colors, fonts, and other design elements.

By 1994, when Web page design had become a minor art form in its own right, hip designers began to hanker (very vocally) for more control over the design, color, and layout of their pages. Although the people in charge of formal HTML standards resisted this pressure, Netscape began to indulge them with a whole series of new tags known as "Netscape extensions," which were primarily concerned with making pages look attractive rather than ensuring that their content was portable between computers.

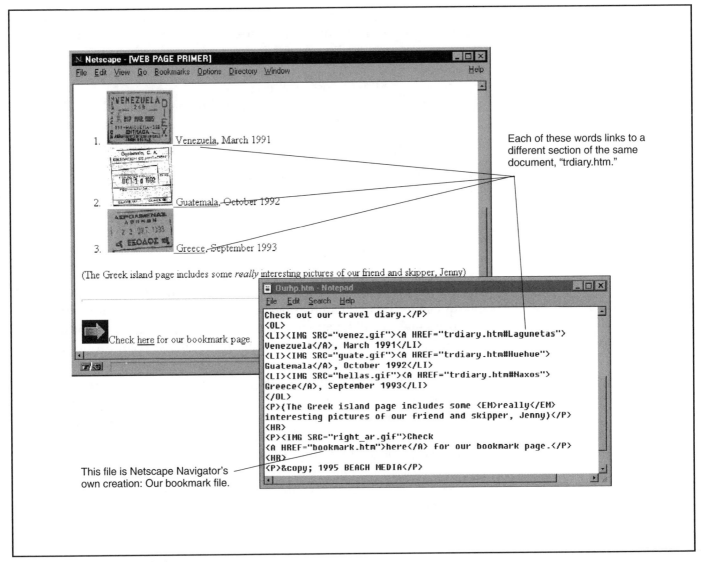

Figure 7-6: *Creating text links.*

Our pictures are now "clickable."

These are full-size pictures of us that can be downloaded.

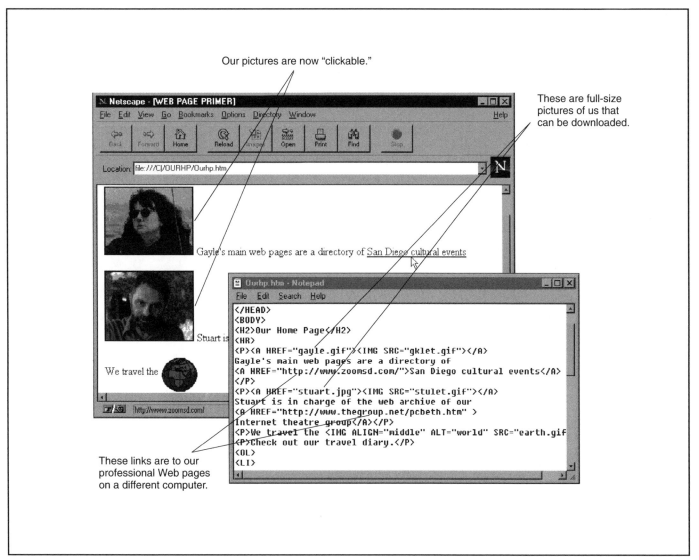

These links are to our professional Web pages on a different computer.

Figure 7-7: *Creating more complex links.*

When you see a Web page with a note on it such as "Netscape 2.0 compliant"—and that's fairly often, these days—it signals that the page author makes use of some of these designer tags which Netscape Navigator interprets but most other graphical browsers do not. To give you a little flavor of this new direction HTML seems to be taking, we've used some HTML extensions to enhance our home page somewhat in Figure 7-8, centering the main header, prettying up the horizontal rule, and defining the color we would like the text and background to be (users can still choose to override the color rendering with their own ideas).

HOT TIP

Those color codes like "#e6e6fa" for lavender are actually just a way of defining a color in terms of the amount of red, blue, and green in it. Since 256 levels of each color are available, you can specify over 16 million different colors with these codes. What makes them a bit hard to grasp is that the color levels are written in a type of computer arithmetic called hexadecimal. Here are a few more to choose from:

```
#000000  Black        #ff00ff  Magenta
#ffffff  White        #ffff00  Yellow
#ff0000  Red          #a52a2a  Brown
#00ff00  Green        #ff7256  Coral
#0000ff  Blue         #6b8e23  Olive
#00ffff  Cyan         #deb887  Tan
```

There are color swatches in many places on the Web, allowing you to pick attractive colors by their #rrggbb codes. One good one is at: **http://www.vmedia.com/alternate/vvc/onlcomp/hpia/colors.html**.

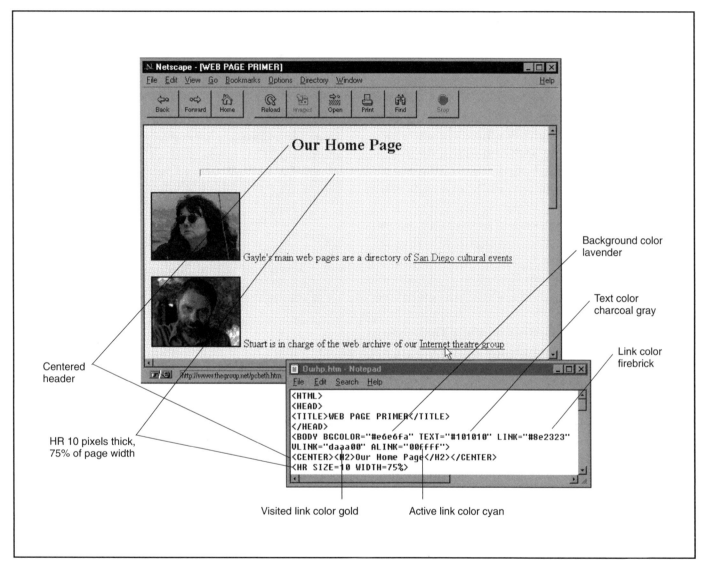

Figure 7-8: *Getting a bit stylish.*

Labels on figure:

Background color lavender

Text color charcoal gray

Link color firebrick

Centered header

HR 10 pixels thick, 75% of page width

Visited link color gold

Active link color cyan

Netscape window content:

Our Home Page

Gayle's main web pages are a directory of San Diego cultural events

Stuart is in charge of the web archive of our Internet theatre group

http://www.thegroup.net/pcbeth.htm

Notepad window — Ourhp.htm:

```
<HTML>
<HEAD>
<TITLE>WEB PAGE PRIMER</TITLE>
</HEAD>
<BODY BGCOLOR="#e6e6fa" TEXT="#101010" LINK="#8e2323"
VLINK="daaa00" ALINK="00ffff">
<CENTER><H2>Our Home Page</H2></CENTER>
<HR SIZE=10 WIDTH=75%>
```

How We Raided the Louvre...
And They'll Never Catch Us!

Remember how we mentioned, back in Chapter 1, that the Web is a free-for-all that makes copyright attorneys wake up screaming in the night? And back in Chapter 2, the fact that the WebMuseum pages are renowned for good design? Put those two facts together and you have the background to a daringly successful raid we carried out on the Louvre one day.

We were wondering how to draw an icon to use as a link to our travel diary, when we saw the WebMuseum page (then known as the Web Louvre) depicted in Figure 7-9. "What a nice icon," we thought. And then we thought, just like many art thieves must have thought, "Hmmm . . . would look swell in our collection." Figure 7-10 shows what we were after.

So we waited until the dead of night, Paris time (it helped that they were eight hours ahead), and then returned to that Web page. Moving silently but efficiently, we stroked our mouse pointer oh so gently against that little picture we craved.

Working quickly now, afraid to hear the words *"mais, Monsieur, Madame . . . ooh la-la! Qu'est-ce que vous faites?"* we clicked the right mouse button and brought up the menu shown in Figure 7-11, which makes it so easy to commit the final act of "larceny" that it would seem a shame to let it escape. Another swift stroke of the mouse, and the prize was ours. All that remained was to decide, as Figure 7-12 shows, what to call our booty. We settled on the default "**earth.gif,**" and the rest you know.

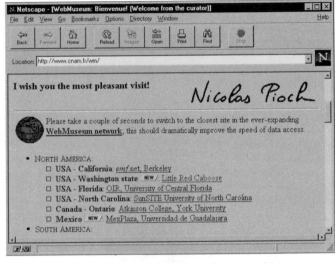

Figure 7-9: *Something caught our eye in the WebMuseum . . .*

Figure 7-10: *The little icon we decided to "steal."*

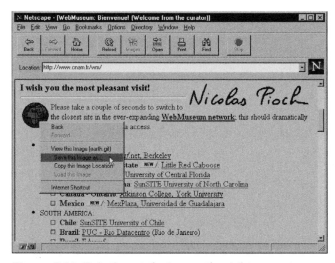

Figure 7-11: *Pointing at the image, the right mouse button allows us to grab it.*

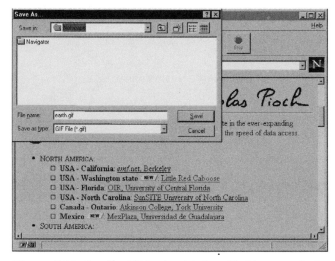

Figure 7-12: *"earth.gif" is about to be added to our private collection.*

A Copyright Caution

As you can see, we take a rather lighthearted view of Web copyright, but that does not mean we disregard copyright altogether, or would advise you to. We always put a copyright notice on our pages, and we'd certainly be annoyed if somebody took the entire content and design of one of our pages and claimed it as his or her own. We'd only be *really* mad if something we designed as a public service was used commercially for profit by someone else. But the Web was founded on the principle of free and open exchange and it doesn't do to further the cause to be constantly looking over our shoulders. If we put little icons and designs out there, we consider them fair game (the lawyers would use the term "fair use") and the overwhelming majority of Web authors would agree.

Before you take anything from the Web for your own use, take a look around and see if the author claims copyright. If so—and many do—consider what exactly the author wants to defend. The icons? The overall design? Certain specific contents? If you're unsure about reusing anything, send e-mail to the page's author and ask. At the very least, it's considered the polite thing to do and most will be flattered.

We're quite confident that our tongue-in-cheek "raid" would not offend Nicolas Pioch because, although he claims copyright on the WebMuseum, he makes his attitude quite clear on his own copyright page in which he (also tongue slightly in cheek) grants a license for fair use. Read it for yourself at: **http://www.emf.net/wm/about/license.html**.

Testing Your Page

As you can see, we've composed our page using nothing but a simple text editor (Windows Notepad), and for simple Web page design you need nothing more. However, fancier Web page design can get much more complicated, and it's often hard to remember to put all the right code in the right places. Those who get serious about Web page design generally find that dedicated or specialized HTML editors are worthwhile to simplify the job and reduce frustration.

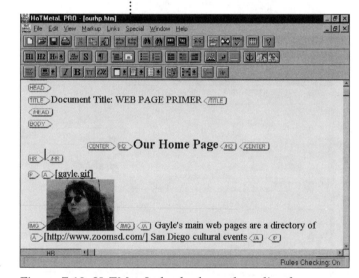

Figure 7-13: *HoTMetaL clearly shows the coding for our page.*

One top-of-the-line editor is HoTMetaL. As you're composing, HoTMetaL will prompt you for the appropriate codes and let you know if you're violating rules of HTML composition. Even when we've composed our page with a text editor and it looks good on Netscape Navigator, we find it good practice to test the page by loading it into HoTMetaL. (See Figure 7-13.) If HoTMetaL finds something wrong, it will tell you what it thinks the problem is. There's a good chance that if HoTMetaL has problems, some other Web browser will have problems too.

There are a number of other shareware editors also available on the Web. You'll find reference to them at many Web development sites and in the Usenet news groups dedicated to Web authoring.

Dan Connolly of Hal Computer Systems offers a free online HTML checking service at: **http://www.hal.com/users/connolly/html-test/service**.

When you get to Dan's page, you just enter, in the box provided, the URL of the code you want checked, and it reports back any errors or inconsistencies it finds. WebLint, another online HTML editing aid, will check any HTML document you've created for coding problems and let you know what you should do to fix it. Its address is: **http://www.unipress.com/web-lint**.

If you intend to post your page for public access on the Web, it's important to remember that not everyone on the Web has Netscape Navigator. Navigator is very forgiving, but some other Web browsers can be very fussy. If at all possible, you should try viewing your page with other browsers (any of the various flavors of Mosaic, for example). You should also consider the users without graphical interfaces who will see your page as pure text. You can test-view your page with the textual browser, Lynx, which you can access online. It's also a good idea to see what it looks like on different machines.

Of course, all of this is irrelevant if you've just designed your page for your own amusement and private use (and you can always send it to friends). For truly professional Web page design, you should engage a professional. Accessing databases, using image maps, devising proper forms for two-way information, and ensuring security is a whole 'nother kettle of fish.

Online HTML Editing Guides   Anyone interested in delving further into HTML composition can find lots of HTML guides and reference material on the Web. For the authoritative information, go straight to HTML's birthplace at the European Laboratory for Particle Physics (CERN), where the father of HTML himself, Tim Berners-Lee, has posted the HTML Style Guides, as well as a number of other HTML reference documents:

http://www.w3.org/hypertext/WWW/Provider/Style/Overview.html

A good HTML FAQ can be found at:

http://sunsite.unc.edu/boutell/faq/www_faq.html

You can create simple HTML documents online and save them to your own computer with the EasyHTML editor at:

http://peachpit.ncsa.uiuc.edu:80/easyhtml/

Posting Your Page

So you think the whole world should know about the wonderful page you've just designed, huh? The spirit of the Internet, after all, is that anyone can participate and there are no taste arbiters deciding who can and can't be part of it. Practically speaking, though, posting your page for public access is a lot more complicated on the World Wide Web, unless you're hooked up to a major academic or big business server—in which case all anyone needs is your URL address to get to your page.

If your page comes under the category of public service—information that the public at large might use—you may find a community bulletin board that would include it in their postings or an access provider who is willing to post it free to enhance his or her own service. Look for start-up access providers—they're often pleased to find interesting Web pages to help put their brand new sites on the map.

If your page has a business or commercial aspect, there are plenty of access providers who would be happy to post it for you for a fee, and given the competitive nature of the business right now, the fees can be quite reasonable. Web business is a lively, developing field—check around and see what you can turn up. Some access providers now offer basic Web page posting space included in their access fees, or for a modest add-on fee.

Web Page Design Tips

Good Web page design is largely a matter of common sense. Nothing is more irritating to Web browsers than coming across a huge document with multiple links and numerous inline images that takes several minutes to download onto your system before you discover that it's not what you want at all.

Here are some useful things to remember:

- Close all your statements—usually an <X> needs a </X>. The few exceptions include <P>, <LI>, <HR>, and <IMG>.

- Keep your inline images small—under 25K is a good guide. All six of the little inline images we used in our demonstration page totaled less than 50K, and the page loads in a few seconds.

- Offer a link to larger images and if they're very large files (over 75K), tell readers how large they are.

- Never use an inline image wider than 600 pixels. Web users expect to scroll vertically but they'll hate you for making them scroll horizontally.

- Break large documents into smaller files logically. They'll load faster and be easier to use.

- Make sure your hyperlinks have full addresses.

- Test your page and all its links. If possible, test it with different browsers and on different computers.

- Describe your document accurately in the title, and resist the temptation to be too cute. The title is frequently used by Web searchers to find topics on the Web.

- Keep it simple. As in all good design, less is more.

Moving On

With the simple basics we've given you in this chapter, we hope you'll have fun creating your own documents. If nothing else, it could be a great party showoff—and perhaps slightly more entertaining than home videos of your latest trip (depending on your taste).

In the next chapter we'll talk about some specialized Web applications. We'll dig into the wealth of reference materials available on the Web and toss up some of the more useful gems. We'll look at the various search engines and how you can find out what's available on the Web on any topic you're interested in. And finally, we'll give you some more neat pages you can visit as you continue your journeys on the Web with Netscape Navigator.

SEARCHING & SITES

Now that you've had a chance to see what the Web has to offer, it's highly likely you're eager to find your own particular interests—be they recreational, business, or research oriented. Finding that special something is not always an easy job, particularly because the Web changes every day. Make that every minute!

We'll devote much of this chapter to the task of searching the Web. We'll explain what kind of searches you can do and how to construct a search. Then we'll look at what some of our favorite search engines do and compare their results.

Then it's time for some Web-sailing. We'll leave you with a list of our favorite Web sites—prize-winning pages, repositories of great information, or just-plain-fun stuff.

Web Searching Tips

The first thing to realize about search engines on the Web is that not all searchers are created equal. The types of data they look for and the kinds of searches they do can be very different. One searcher may look for keywords in the titles of documents only, another will search all hypertext citation links in documents for the keyword. Still a third will search the entire text of the documents in its base.

In the latter case, you can see how a lot of irrelevant information can be thrown up. This is especially so if it is searching for a string instead of a word. Say you typed in "bee" for a keyword. If it's searching for the string it will find "beer" and "has-been" and "beetroot" and who knows what else.

Another difference in search engines is the extent to which they allow you to qualify your search, since obviously the more you can qualify it, the better your chances of getting exactly what you want. Most searchers encourage you to put as many keywords as you think relevant in your search, but this is not always helpful—it may simply turn up more irrelevant documents rather than relevant ones.

Here are the basic types of searches possible, each followed by an example. Bear in mind that not all searchers are capable of all of them.

- **Simple keyword search**: killer bee
  This will return all documents containing either the word "killer" and/or "bee."

- **Boolean query**: bee AND killer
  This looks for occurrences of both words in a document, in any order.

- **Phrase query**: "killer bee"
  This will return all documents that contain "killer bee" as a phrase.

You can also devise even more complex searches, such as:

- **Boolean queries with phrases**: "killer bee" AND California
- **Simple structured query**: Title: "killer bee"
  This will only return documents that have "killer bee" in the Title.
- **Complex query**: California AND (Title: "killer bee")
  This will return documents that have "killer bee" in the title and "California" in the body.

No matter what you do, expect a few surprises. When we tried this out, our search for "killer bee" threw up, unexpectedly, a rock band called The Killer Bees and a NASA computer dubbed the killerbee.

Now that we've shown you some basic types of searches, here are some fundamental things to keep in mind when searching:

- Know what kind of citations the searcher is looking for. Read the Help screens and FAQs before you start.
- Be as specific as you can.
- Use OR to widen your search. Use AND to narrow it.
- Don't use words that are too general or too common. The documentation for one Web searcher points out that "to be or not to be" is reduced to nothing by its initial keyword processing.
- Don't use plural forms or weird declensions.
- Realize that sometimes all it takes is a few good hits, as similar documents on a subject may well link to each other.
- Remember where you've been. Take notes if necessary.

Is There Life on Mars?

One of the most thumbed sections of our bookmark list is the "Web Searchers" category. Like everyone else, we have research needs both formal (providing biology abstracts for non-Net-savvy clients) and informal (what was that address for the Paris Metro route planner?).

There are dozens of Web searchers available for your use, several of which you can get to via your Net Search directory button. To review our three favorite searchers in some coherent way for this book, we asked them if there was life on Mars. We had bacteria in mind rather than Little Green Men—wouldn't want you to think we're a pair of flakes.

The WebCrawler

Our favorite searcher because it's so easy and quick, the WebCrawler started life as Brian Pinkerton's research project at the University of Washington. It was bought in 1995 by America Online, and now lives at this swanky address in San Francisco:

http://webcrawler.com/

Figure 8-1 shows the Crawler's inquiry screen with those pull-down menus we love to use to switch between an AND search and an OR search or to limit the search if we just want a starting point rather than the full reference desk treatment.

Note that we didn't enter "Life on Mars" as our search string—two-letter words like on, at, and in are quite rightly ignored by every searcher. Also, the order and case of words is irrelevant, so "mars life" is as good as "life Mars" or "MARs lIfE."

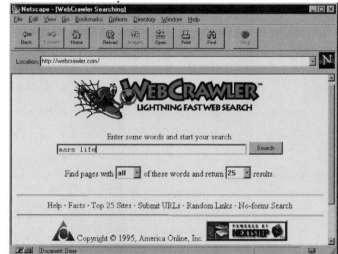

Figure 8-1: *The famous WebCrawler.*

The Crawler does not search the Web itself when you ask it about life on Mars (or anything else). Instead it searches its own *index* of the Web, which is derived from a search of some two million documents. The index is updated every week or so.

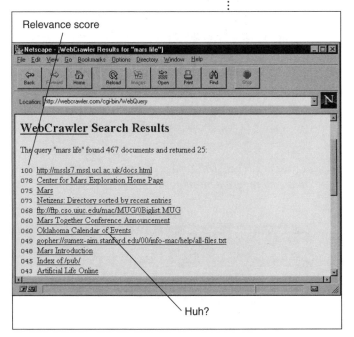

Figure 8-2: *The WebCrawler finds life on Mars.*

Success!

We hit the Search button, and in less than six seconds, the Crawler was back with 467 hits, listing only the first 25 as we'd asked. Figure 8-2 shows the type of list the Crawler spits out: No synopses, just a down-and-dirty list of hyperlinks, with a relevance score beside each one which indicates how well the hit matched your search criteria on a scale of 0-100.

We *loved* number two on the list—the Center for Mars Exploration (see Figure 8-3). This was exactly what we wanted, and included links to everywhere else on the Internet where we could find ammunition for both sides of the argument. The Lunar and Planetary Lab of the University of Arizona has a great page, too, including a gorgeous picture and a hyperlink to the music from Holst's *The Planets* Suite. This page is actually part of a multimedia tour of all nine planets. A Stanford University Conference Announcement, number six on the list, was also of interest. So for us, this was a typically successful Web search—very fast, with plenty of goodies.

Strange Results From the Web

There's no such thing as a *perfect* search, however, and this one was no exception. We'll never know how good items one, four, and five were, because they were all outdated and the links to them failed. We were amused by the inclusion, further down the list, of the Internet Anagram Server. It's wittily entitled "Inert Grave Near Mars," and it includes the quote "All life's wisdom can be found in anagrams." Serendipity like that is a feature of all search engines, there being no way on Earth a computer could know that this was an inappropriate hit.

What about the Oklahoma Calendar of Events, though? What's *that* doing in the list? Well, "Mars" is an interesting word to a computer that's been taught to ignore plural forms, particularly to one that hasn't been told that substrings (partial words) are not okay. So, as Figure 8-4 shows, the WebCrawler was happy to tell us that an exhibition of wildLIFE photography was happening MAR 2-26 not far from the Flea MARket. "MARk your calendars now," advised the page. Shucks, we missed it . . .

Yahoo

http://www.yahoo.com/

Ever wonder what would happen if you just kept building and building your bookmark list forever? Maybe you'd become the most popular Internet directory of all, with 15 million inquiries a week using your cataloging skills. Then you'd be set up by the Netscape Communications Corporation with an office and a suite of high-powered computers, quit your Ph.D. program to devote yourself to the list full-time, and live happily ever after.

Figure 8-3: *The CMEX page: All we ever wanted to know and maybe a bit more.*

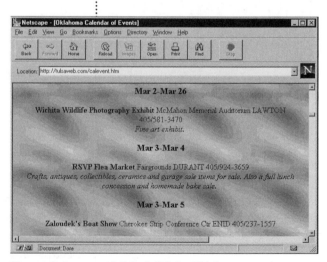

Figure 8-4: *. . . and there's life in Oklahoma too, it seems.*

Far-fetched, you think? That's exactly what happened to Stanford University electrical engineering students David Filo and Jerry Yang, who started "Yet Another Hierarchical, Officious Oracle" on their lab workstations in March 1994. A year later they went full-time on what was by then a mega-list, vowing that success would not spoil Yahoo (but hinting commercials were going to become part of it one day).

Yahoo is also an index, but it's browsable as well as searchable. Following the front page links to Science/astronomy brought us to the same good pages as the Crawler had found fairly quickly. These site lists are an absolute model of efficiency, and very up-to-date. However, entering search keywords was not as successful—we ended up with the home page of someone called Kathy Mar and a reference to Sweetwater MARSh National WildLIFE Refuge (which, as it so happens, is just down the road from us).

If you click on the word "Options" beside Yahoo's Search button, you get the chance to refine your search in several ways, including telling it you don't want substrings.

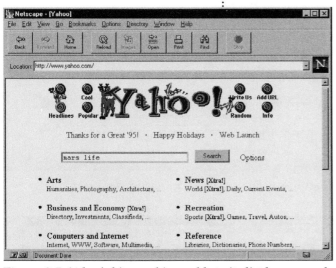

Figure 8-5: *Yahoo's hip graphics and hot site list have earned it a huge following.*

Lycos

http://lycos.cs.cmu.edu

The Washington WebCrawler was not only our favorite in terms of convenience, but also the best—until Lycos came along. Lycos—a whole array of hardware and software at Carnegie-Mellon University, Pittsburgh—is super-duper. Like the WebCrawler, it keeps its own local index for search speed, but it also fetches new documents "on the fly" and adds them into its ever-burgeoning indexes. The larger of the two principal catalogs indexed its ten millionth URL in October 1995.

Okay, Lycos is a tiny bit slower than the Crawler—but it is much more thorough. Lycos has the interesting philosophy of scoring a citation higher if it comes up in the first paragraph of a document. It is also superior when it comes to Boolean searches and "regular expressions." If you enter "mars." it will understand the period to mean that you are only interested in the whole word, not things like flea markets.

Figure 8-6 gives an idea of the inventive ways you can customize a Lycos search. Tell it how good you want the match to be, for instance, on the scale "loose/fair/good/close/strong." A "mars. life" search took 11 seconds with loose matching and located 55,957 documents with at least one of the search words. It displayed the first 20 of the 256 it considered a good match.

Figure 8-7 shows the excellent synopsis Lycos provides on its hits—that's one way in which it differs from the WebCrawler and Yahoo. Another way is that, no matter what the subject, Lycos always seems to come up with entirely different pages. That's why our advice is "don't ever rely on just one searcher."

Search Engines à Gogo

There's certainly no shortage of searchers to choose from. There are about a dozen in our Netscape Navigator bookmark list, and more seem to spring up every day—although some that claim to be new actually turn out to be "meta-indexes," meaning, indexes of indexes. On these pages you can pass your keyword search to many different search engines without

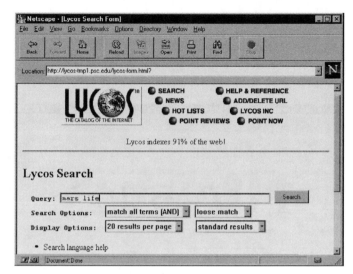

Figure 8-6: *Lycos allows very sophisticated searching.*

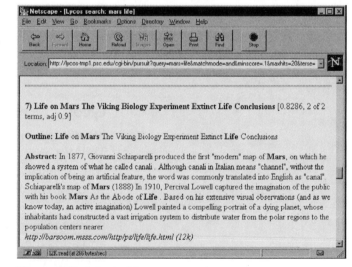

Figure 8-7: *A typical Lycos synopsis.*

moving. We don't particularly recommend this approach—it has the appearance of being convenient, but the "shortcuts" offered to each searcher seem to bypass many of the options that would make your search more logical. How hard is it to go to the indexes themselves rather than a meta-index?

Here, in no particular order, are some of the others we use less often than our "top three."

The World Wide Web Worm
http://www.cs.colorado.edu/home/mcbryan/WWWW.html

Infoseek
http://www2.infoseek.com

CUI Web Catalog
http://cuiwww.unige.ch/

Aliweb
http://www.cs.indiana.edu/aliweb/search

Jump Station II
http://www.stir.ac.uk/jsbin/js

The Harvest Access System
http://www.town.hall.org/brokers/www-home-pages/query.html

Searching Usenet Archives

If there's one information resource that rivals the Web in terms of quantity of information it's Usenet news. Figure 8-8 shows the search form of an outfit called DejaNews, all ready to go find another of our favorite topics—the wines of Burgundy. Figure 8-9 shows the results from searching thousands of newsgroup articles going back many months. Not bad.

A subsidiary page of the DejaNews service allows you to set a "query filter." This might be "only search these newsgroups," "look for articles by this author," or "search from 15th March to 15th June."

Exploring Cyberspace

The day when dry tomes from the catacombs of science and esoteric discussions of quarks dominated the Web is long gone. There are still tons of good references for real and would be scientists on the Web—in fact, they form a strong backbone to the system. But the diversity of resources devoted to the wide range of human interests is expanding daily on the Web.

Among the types of Web sites you can visit now are electronic newspapers and magazines, museums and art galleries, entertainment resources, business and commercial outlets, along with many sites run by government, academic, or private institutions sharing their own special databases and information.

To give you a feel for the diversity of the Web, we've collected some outstanding sites in various categories. We've even made it easy for you by including them in our *Netscape Navigator Quick Tour for Windows Online Companion*. Go to **http://www.vmedia.com/nqt.html** and you'll find hypertext links to these and other Web resources. Take them as starting points and then wander at will. To quote Dr. Seuss, "Oh, the places you'll go!"

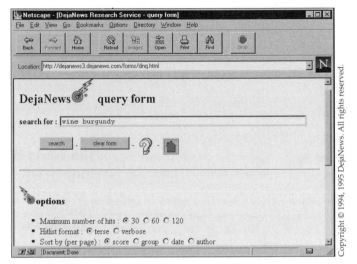

Figure 8-8: *DejaNews's input screen.*

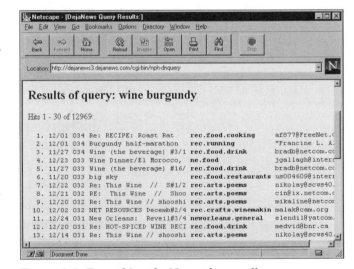

Figure 8-9: *Everything the Usenet has to offer on Burgundy, retrieved in a jiffy.*

Electronic Publications

Time-Life Publishing

http://www.timeinc.com/pathfinder/

Here you can find an online edition of *Time* magazine with excerpts from the latest issue, as well as excerpts from several other Time-Life-owned magazines, such as *Southern Living, Sunset,* and *Entertainment Weekly.* You can choose a high- or low-speed version to suit your taste and computer capacity.

Hotwired

http://www.wired.com

Hotwired is the online version of *Wired* magazine, where all the techno-hip cognoscenti hang out. The graphics in its online edition are really exceptional, and the publication is state-of-the-art in Web publishing.

Ecola Design Newsstand

http://www.ecola.com/ez/frames.htm

A whole host of newspapers and magazines are jumping into the online publishing arena. The Ecola Design Newsstand is a very attractive site making use of Netscape's FRAMES procedure to split the screen and display some very interesting wares. *Elle, The Economist,* and *Der Spiegel* are here. So is *People* and many, many others.

Nando.net

http://www.nando.net/

Nando.net includes an excellent list of online newspapers maintained by the News and Observer Publishing Company. Among the news sources with links to this page are *USA Today,* the *San Francisco*

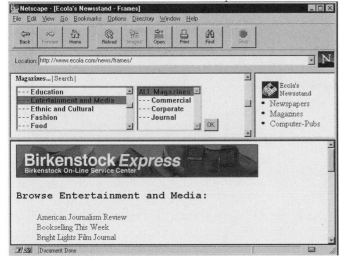

Figure 8-10: *Ecola's Online Newsstand: Not just attractive, useful as well.*

Chronicle & Examiner, San Jose Mercury News, Boston Globe, St. Petersburg Press, CBC, CNN Headline News, and the (London) *Times* literary supplement. This is a subscription service, but the cost is very low.

International & Other News Links

For international news links, go to
http://www.cs.vu.nl/~gerben/news.html

Some other newspapers and magazines to peruse are:
Boardwatch: **http://www.boardwatch.com**
VIBE: **http://www.timeinc.com/vibe/VibeOnline!.html**
Washington Weekly: **http://dolphin.gulf.net**
Wall Street Journal: **http://www.wsj.com/**
PC Week and *PC Magazine:* **http://www.ziff.com**
San Francisco Examiner/Chronicle:
http://www.sfgate.com/
Private Eye (British satirical):
http://www.intervid.co.uk/intervid/eye/gateway.html

Sports

Sports news and the latest scores in football, basketball, baseball, hockey, and soccer are a popular resource at The World Wide Web of Sports:
http://www.tns.lcs.mit.edu/cgi-bin/sports

Nando.net also has a super sports site (and this is on the house) at:
http://www2.nando.net/SportServer/

The latest tennis rankings and results can be found at:
http://www.tennisserver.com/

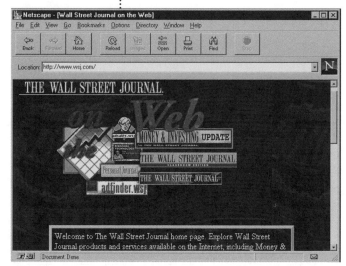

Figure 8-11: *The Wall Street Journal's smart-looking home page.*

Museums & Art Galleries

WebMuseum, Paris
http://mistral.enst.fr/wm/net/
Nicolas Pioch, who maintains this page, had to stop calling it "Le WebLouvre" after an icy letter from lawyers representing the Ministry of Cultural Affairs. *Lese majesté* notwithstanding, this is the model that many other museums are trying to follow as they go online. See highlights of exhibits at the Louvre in Paris and as an added attraction, take a "walking tour" of Paris. Nobody knows a good tourist lure like the Parisians.

There are many mirror sites all over the world, and the idea is to relieve the immense load on the original computer in Paris. On the east coast of the United States, there's **http://sunsite.unc.edu/wm**, and we Californians should (and do) use **http://www.emf.net/wm** at Berkeley.

The Smithsonian
http://www.si.edu
Visit the Smithsonian Institution in Washington, DC, and you'll find a wealth of resources for teachers, students, and the aimlessly curious. You can access the National Museum of Natural History, the National Air and Space Museum, and the Smithsonian Education Server from here.

London's Natural History Museum
http://www.nhm.ac.uk/
A heavy-duty site but why not? It's one of the major museums in the world, the home of Charles Darwin and friends. It contains extensive information on the museum's science programs and collections on earth and life sciences, and the flora and fauna of MesoAmerica, among other things.

The Exploratorium

http://www.exploratorium.edu

The online interface of this many-faceted museum in the Palace of Fine Arts in San Francisco is a labyrinth for exploring science and nature topics.

Expo

http://sunsite.unc.edu/expo/expo/busstation.html

Tour six expositions organized by the Library of Congress with links to other major museum sites via the virtual shuttle bus. See the Soviet Archive Exhibit, the 1492 Exhibit, the Paleontology Exhibit, the Vatican Exhibit, the Dead Sea Scrolls Exhibit, or the Spalato Exhibit exploring the palace of Diocletian at Split.

Restaurant Le Cordon Bleu

http://sunsite.unc.edu/expo/restaurant/restaurant.html

The Restaurant Le Cordon Bleu is a sidestop on the Expo museum tour. It includes a pictorial gourmet menu for each day of the week, with accompanying recipes from the cookbook *Le Cordon Bleu at Home.*

ArtServe

http://rubens.anu.edu.au/

Australian National University offers a comprehensive overview of their collections focusing on art history. This site provides access to some 2,800 images of prints, from the 15th century to the 19th century, including some 2,500 images of classical architecture and sculpture from around the Mediterranean.

Art Crimes
http://www.gatech.edu/desoto/graf/Index.Art_Crimes.html
Graffiti around the world. Whoever thought a can of spray paint could be so creative? Seriously though, some of this is untutored native genius, others represent art in public places by serious artists.

Last Files From the News
http://www.cnam.fr/Images/Usenet/
Every day brings a hundred or so new pieces of computer art, from space pictures to "my wife streaking a hotel corridor" (we're not making this up, folks). Even if you have one of the super newsreaders that downloads and uudecodes them hands-off, the problem still is deciding what's worth your time. This French Web page provides a buffet of all the latest, on a pick 'n' click basis.

Educational Resources

The Education Center
http://crusher.bev.net:80/education/index.html
The Education Center offers dozens of resources for teachers, students, and home-schoolers with new projects being added constantly. Teachers can visit the K-12 Teacher's Lounge and exchange projects and information.

Curry School of Education
http://curry.edschool.virginia.edu
The Curry School at the University of Virginia is dedicated to encouraging interactive education with computers for kids. This is another rich source of educational materials for elementary and high school teachers and students.

Sea World/Busch Gardens

http://crusher.bev.net:80/education/SeaWorld

Sea World maintains a great animal database, which is useful for both teachers and students.

Virtual Frogs

http://george.lbl.gov/ITG.hm.pg.docs/dissect/info.html
http://curry.edschool.virginia.edu/~insttech/frog

It had to happen: dissecting cyberfrogs. Two sites have actually come up with their demo projects for school use, one run by Lawrence Berkeley Laboratories, the other by Curry School at the University of Virginia. Try your lab skills at each of these two sites.

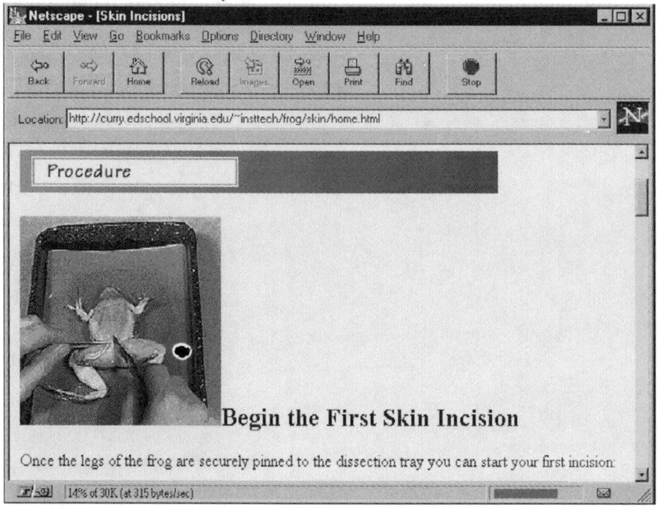

The SILS Clearinghouse

http://www.lib.umich.edu/chhome.html

The University of Michigan's School of Information and Library Studies maintains an ongoing reference called the Clearinghouse for Subject-Oriented Internet Resource Guides. This is a collection of specially-written documents categorized under Humanities, Sciences, Ecology, etc. All of them are lavishly hyperlinked to other Net resources, and anybody can create their own document and submit it for inclusion in this wonderful educational Web page.

Figure 8-12: *The Web must have already saved the lives of a few thousand frogs.*

Kid's Web

http://www.primenet.com/~sburr/index.html

Uncle Bob has one of the best resources on the Web of pages for kids. Lots of educational as well as fun stuff.

Welcome to the Globewide Network Academy
http://uu-gna.mit.edu:8001/uu-gna/
If you can earn a degree by mail, why not by e-mail? This unique site is the first cyberuniversity—a project by a consortium of educational and research organizations dedicated to devising a complete online university.

Government & Institutions

U.S. Government Federal Web Locator
http://www.law.vill.edu/Fed-Agency/fedwebloc.html
We can't express it better than the page itself:
> *The Federal Web Locator is a service provided by the Villanova Center for Information Law and Policy and is intended to be the one stop shopping point for federal government information on the World Wide Web. This list is maintained to bring the cyber citizen to the federal government's doorstep.*

You can even get your tax forms by e-mail.

The White House
http://www.whitehouse.gov
If it's the "Prez" you're interested in, you can skip the previous page and go straight to the White House. Take a tour of the interior or see The Man himself at play with the family cat—who looks like she'd rather be in Arkansas.

The Constitution of the United States of America
http://www.law.cornell.edu/constitution/constitution.overview.html
Want to check on your Constitutional rights? The entire Constitution is easily accessible online, thanks to Cornell University Law School.

NASA

http://hypatia.gsfc.nasa.gov/NASA_homepage.html

Seems every Net jockey in the world is interested in rockets and space-ships. NASA's home pages are among the most visited on the Web. Here you can get the latest news on space shuttle missions and view some of the wealth of space imagery generated by NASA's activities. Your best start on the monster that is NASA is the home page at Goddard Space-flight Center—it provides links to all the other NASA sites.

Web-related Institutions

The Internet Society

http://www.isoc.org

The international body that considers all the weighty issues concerned with keeping the Internet up and running has its home page here, with links to important documents and discussion of current Internet- and Web-related issues.

The Internet Engineering Task Force (IETF)

http://www.ietf.cnri.reston.va.us/home.html

Computer and industry experts gather here to discuss technical issues of Internet development and maintenance. Their three-times-a-year meetings are open to the public, as are the archives they maintain to invite public discussion.

The World Wide Web Consortium

http://www.w3.org

The W3 Consortium, as it's known, is a collaborative project between the Massachusetts Institute of Technology and CERN to promote Web standards. They maintain an archive of information for Web developers and users, including all the latest HTML references. If you need the authoritative word on HTML, you'll find it here.

The Electronic Frontier Foundation

http://www.eff.org/

The Electronic Frontier Foundation is a nonprofit civil liberties public interest organization working to protect freedom of expression, privacy, and access to online resources and information. For serious discussions of these developing issues, see this page.

Business & Commercial

Open Market Inc.

http://www.directory.net

Visit the Open Market for a directory of commercial services, products, and information on the Internet. See What's New or search for a product on the Net. Our search for "flowers" turned up 13 online florists.

Interesting Business Sites

http://www.rpi.edu/~okeefe/business.html

The businesses in this list are personally selected by Bob O'Keefe at the School of Management, Rensselaer Polytechnic Institute, and updated monthly. He keeps a keen eye out for the latest business developments on the Net.

Stock Market Updates

http://www.secapl.com

Several services offer stock quotes and market rates online. For a fee, a number of them allow you to register your portfolio to receive closing prices every day. We like the site run by Security APL Inc., which as a come-on to their services lets you get free quotes, one at a time. Their Market Watch Page is updated every three minutes during trading hours.

Databases

U.S. Census Information Server
http://www.census.gov/

The Census Bureau posts population statistics; financial data on state and local governments and schools; county and city data; and census bureau publications.

Zip+4 Lookup
http://www.usps.gov/ncsc/lookups/
lookup_zip+4.html

Another U.S. Government agency that's making good use of the Web is the postal service. At this site, you can enter an address and get its zip+4.

The Human Genome Project
http://gdbwww.gdb.org/

The Human Genome Project has taken on the monumental task of mapping every chromosome and writing down the complete genetic code that describes a human being, letter by letter. Scientists and medical specialists around the world access this database, which is constantly being updated. The effort is split between several Web sites, but this is the best one for understanding the database.

Global Job Net
http://www.globaljobnet.com/

The Global Job Net is a giant database functioning as a job/resume matching service.

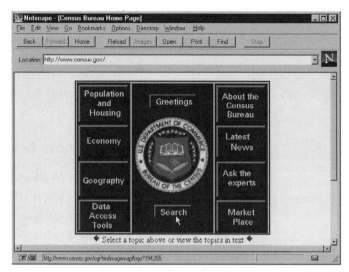

Figure 8-13: *The Census page.*

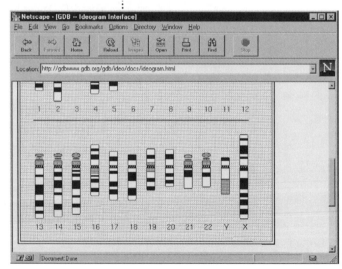

Figure 8-14: *Genetic databases, like these chromosome marker maps, could hardly be better suited for Internet access.*

Genealogy

There are literally thousands of computer-accessible genealogy databases out there. GenWeb claims to bring all of them to a single site. Access at:

http://www.doit.com/tdoyle/genweb/

Fly Fishing Database

Recreational databases are all the rage. This is just one we've picked at random:

http://www.geo.mtu.edu/~jsuchosk/fish/ff-faq/masterIndex.html

Movies & Entertainment

The Internet Movie Database

http://www.cm.cf.ac.uk/Movies/

The Internet Movie Database offers pages for film buffs and trivia quiz masters. Search for movie titles, actors, directors, what have you.

Movie Studios

Visit the movie studios and see previews of coming attractions in downloadable QuickTime clips. You can even visit the Press Room for upcoming attractions. Disney (Buena Vista Pictures):

http://bvp.wdp.com:80/index.html

MCA/Universal Pictures "Cyberwalk":

http://www.mca.com/

More Movie Stuff

Hollywood gossip from "Mr. Showbiz":

http://web3.starwave.com/showbiz/

Figure 8-15: *The Internet Movie Database: One of the Web's most popular pages.*

(but you can't beat the Usenet group alt.showbiz.gossip).
Movie page:

http://www.film.com/

Live shot of what's happening at Hollywood & Vine (this one's for dedicated *aficionados* only):

http://hollywood.bhi.hollywood.ca.us:8000/pictures/

MovieLink

http://www.movielink.com

Find out what's playing tonight at your neighborhood movie theatre if you live in one of the dozen or so cities that MovieLink includes in its searchable database.

Travel

The Virtual Tourist

http://www.xmission.com/~kinesava/webmap/

Here you can find virtual tourist guides for countries around the world, as well as a link to a U.S. city guide index called "City.Net." Just click on the world map to see what's available.

The London Guide

http://www.cs.ucl.ac.uk/misc/uk/london.html

This is one of our favorite places to visit when one of us (guess which one) gets homesick. Designed by University College, London, these pages are a resource for Londoners and tourists alike, with guides to the theater scene, pubs, restaurants, hotels, and even a "Tube Journey Planner" that plots your route on the London Underground.

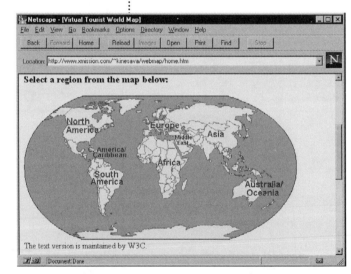

Figure 8-16: *If only travel were this easy . . . Nah, the agony's half the fun!*

The Paris Pages
http://www.paris.org/
A perfect companion to the WebMuseum, the Paris Pages are a complete visitor's guide to Paris—its museums, monuments, special expositions, cafés, restaurants, and sights, as well as practical information like air and rail transportation, the Métro, and hotels. Lots of swell images, too.
   Also try FranceScape at:
http://www.france.com/francescape/top.html

U.S. CityLink
http://www.NeoSoft.com:80/citylink/default.html
This service provides links to information about cities all over the United States, and they're expanding to include international destinations as well. A good resource for travelers.

Travels With Samantha
http://www.swiss.ai.mit.edu/samantha/travels-with-samantha.html
MIT programmer Phil Greenspun's travelogue of his trip around North America with his PowerBook, Samantha, won a Best of the Web '94 award, as much for his beautiful pictures as his personal-style narrative. Be forewarned that you'll need considerable memory to view his high-quality images.

Reference Pages

The Hypertext Webster
http://c.gp.cs.cmu.edu:5103/prog/webster

This is an online searchable index of the Webster's dictionary. Look up any word and get the definition. If you spell it wrong, it will guess at what you mean and prompt you. Definitions are themselves hypertext-linked.

Other Dictionaries
The best list of dictionaries and thesauri is kept by Jürgen Péus in Paderborn, Germany:
http://math-www.uni-paderborn.de/HTML/Dictionaries.html

Carnegie-Mellon Reference Desk
http://www-cgi.cs.cmu.edu/Web/references.html
Another excellent set of librarians' links, including a U.S. area code list, a currency converter, and the CIA World Factbook.

University of Iowa Map Center
http://www.cgrer.uiowa.edu/servers/servers_references.html
This site is a general aid to exploration, but specializes in map collections that are Web-accessible. We followed a hyperlink path to a map of our own beach, and discovered a few things we weren't aware of (Hmmm, in future when we have beach parties of 75 or more, must make a note to get permission from the city.)

Current Weather Maps/Movies
http://clunix.cl.msu.edu:80/weather/
The definitive site for weather maps and information. Find out the weather anywhere in the world and view the latest satellite pictures.

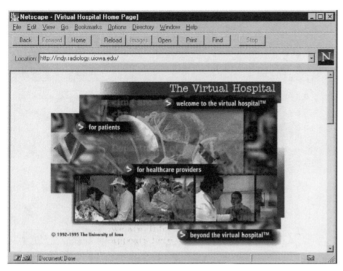

Figure 8-17: *The Virtual Hospital in Iowa.*

The Human Languages Page

http://www.willamette.edu:80/~tjones/Language-Page.html

From Bulgarian poetry to the daily news in Danish, it's all here in this incredible collection of dictionaries and linguistic references.

The Virtual Hospital

http://indy.radiology.uiowa.edu/

The University of Iowa hospital has put a considerable amount of patient information online here for public access. Get information about heart disease, poison control, obstetrics and gynecology, sexually transmitted diseases, and the warning signs of heart attack and stroke.

Personal Home Pages

"Nerd World" Home Page Directory

http://challenge.tiac.net/users/dstein/nw163.html

One of the best ways to discover interesting Web sites is to find out where other Web users are spending their time. If it's cool or interesting, you can bet other people have put it on their private lists. There are far too many personal home pages for a proper directory to exist—let alone stay current—but Nerd World gives it a shot.

Prizewinning Web Pages

The Best of the Web

http://wings.buffalo.edu/contest/awards/index.html
This is the home of the annual Best of the Web Contest which awards Web page designers for outstanding presentations in more than a dozen categories. You'll find links to all the winners as well as runners-up here. It's a great place to see what the state of the art in Web design is these days.

Global Network Navigator

http://gnn.com/gnn/index.html
O'Reilly & Associates, pioneers in the Web, present a wealth of resources on the Net on their extensive home pages, which include links to business pages, Net news, travel, personal finance, and their own picks of the best of the Web.

URouLette

http://www.uroulette.com:8000/
Don't know where you want to go? Let URouLette choose for you. Spin the wheel and you'll be sent off to a random Web address. This recently revamped page is *wildly* popular!

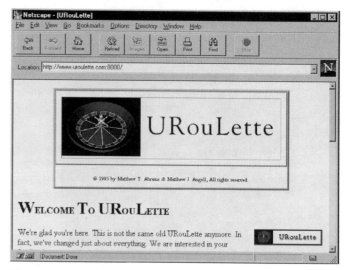

Figure 8-18: *Take a chance and let URouLette add some excitement to your life.*

Moving On

What does the future hold on the Web? Right now it's anyone's guess. A few things are certain: The Web will get bigger, it will be easier to access, and a lot more people will be participating in it. But lots of things are unknown. Who will pay for its development? How much will it all cost? What kind of big businesses will grow out of it? How will it affect our lives?

Businesses large and small, academic institutions, and governments will all have a say in this, but so will each one of us who uses it. The Internet continues to be the most revolutionary democratic forum to come along in hundreds of years.

Now that you've learned to navigate the World Wide Web with Netscape Navigator, you qualify as a full-fledged cybercitizen. Care to venture an opinion?

APPENDIX A
ABOUT THE ONLINE COMPANION

Netscape into the World Wide Web! The *Netscape Navigator Quick Tour for Windows Online Companion* is an informative tool, as well as an annotated software library. It aids in your exploration of the World Wide Web while at the same time supports and enhances the Netscape Navigator Web browser. Sections of the *Netscape Navigator Quick Tour for Windows* book are reproduced and hyperlinked to the exciting WWW sites and tools that they reference. So you can just click on the name of the reference and jump directly to the site you're interested in.

Perhaps one of the most impressive features of the *Netscape Navigator Quick Tour for Windows Online Companion* is its Software Archive. Here you'll find and be able to download the latest versions of all the software mentioned in the book that are freely available on the Internet. This software ranges from Netscape Navigator helper applications such as MPEG Player and Wham, which enhance Navigator's graphics and sound capabilities, to many of your basic Internet essentials such as PCEudora, an e-mail tool, and WSFTP, which allows you to easily transfer files to and from your computer. Also with Ventana Online's helpful description of the software, you'll know exactly what you're getting and why—so you won't download the software only to find you have no use for it.

The *Netscape Navigator Quick Tour for Windows Online Companion* also links you to the Ventana Library, where you will find useful press and jacket information on a variety of Ventana offerings. Plus, you have access to a wide selection of exciting new releases and coming attractions. In addition, Ventana's Online Library allows you to order the books you want.

The *Netscape Navigator Quick Tour for Windows Online Companion* represents Ventana Online's ongoing commitment to offering the most dynamic and exciting products possible. And soon Ventana Online will be adding more services, including more multimedia supplements, searchable indexes, and sections of the book reproduced and hyperlinked to the Internet resources they reference.

To access, connect via the World Wide Web to **http://www.vmedia.com/ nqt.html**.

APPENDIX B
UNDOCUMENTED NETSCAPE FEATURES

Undocumented features are sometimes undocumented because somebody forgot to mention some brilliant piece of code to the technical writing department, and sometimes because nobody thought we'd be interested. The fact is that all software has a few features that aren't noted in the manual—and to be honest, many of them come under the heading of "pranks," also known as "Easter eggs." As Netscape Navigator evolves through the versions, its Easter egg list changes almost as often as its list of genuine features. Here are some we've discovered or heard about on the Netscape grapevine. A few of them, including the first on the list, are features that were useful during development and never intended for release.

The File of Files

Create a file in your Netscape Navigator directory called #FILE.HTM. The content of this file can be anything you choose—it doesn't matter. Now start Navigator and Open #FILE.HTM as a local file, as though for HTML editing. You'll find your entire directory opens into the Navigator window, with file types identified by icons exactly as they are at an FTP site. You can click on an HTML file to load it—a very useful mode for a quick look at file content.

This mode can even be incorporated in a link like this:
<A HREF="file:///c | /netscape/#file.htm">link object</A>
A click on "link object" will then bring up your directory.

Different Strokes for Different Folks

The following are keyboard alternatives for common commands:

- Backspace acts like PgUp.
- Spacebar acts like PgDn.
- Ctrl-U acts like Ctrl-L to bring up the Location dialog box.
- Ctrl-P launches Print mode, although the File pull-down menu does not indicate it.
- Ctrl-C or Ctrl-Ins performs an Edit/Copy.
- Ctrl-V or Shift-Ins performs an Edit/Paste.
- Ctrl-X or Shift-Del performs an Edit/Cut.
- Ctrl-Alt-T brings up a window of information on Transfer Status. (This is one they keep meaning to remove, but never get around to it.)
- Ctrl-Alt-S makes the status line go away (and return).

Don't Just Sit There, Spit Meteors at Us

The Netscape logo is an active link: click on it and go to the Netscape Communications Corporation home page, or to whatever surprise they have in store this week.

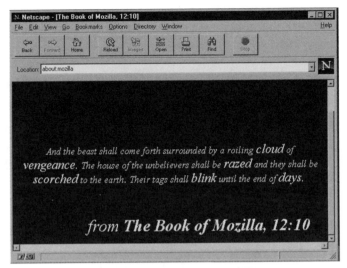

Figure B-1: *Result of entering "about:mozilla" as a URL.*

We Knew That Face was Familiar From Somewhere...

The pseudo-URL "about:" does a few interesting things—the most interesting being the form "about:authors" which brings you a list of Netscape programmers, indicating roughly who did what. We assume Lou Montulli was left on his own in the lab one night, because "about:montulli" is a short cut to the home page of Lou Montulli, author of much of the Netscape code, also principal author of the famous Web browser "Lynx," and—perhaps most important—current guardian of the fishcam (more about this shortly). "Montulli:" on its own reloads something at random from your history list.

Here are some more stupid "about:" tricks:

Pseudo-URL	Result
about:	Same as Help/About
about:document	Same as View/by Document Info
about:mozilla	A reading from the "Book of Mozilla"
about:security?certificate	A list of Netscape's security certification appears.
about:[???]	Try any other string that comes to mind . . .

Go Fish

Netscape's fishcam gives you a continuously-refreshed camera angle on the Netscape aquarium. Apart from being fun, this is also a practical lesson in the document-refresh technique known as "client pull." There's an official way to get to the fishcam via http://home.netscape.com, but Ctrl-Alt-F is a short-cut. Study fish behavior, try and figure how client pull works, and possibly also catch the reflection of Lou Montulli in the front glass. Of course, on days when Lou comes to the office in his Hawaiian shirt, you may not even know you're seeing him!

Beware of Greeks Bearing .GIFs

Browse the *.MOZ files in your cache subdirectory. Some of them will have a GIF87A or GIF89A header. These are images which Netscape Navigator saved in your temporary directory. Rename them as .GIF files to save them permanently.

Why Bother Displaying the Page, When You Can...

go straight to the source code. Simply enter "view-source:" followed by a complete URL.

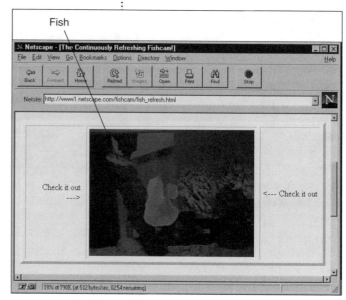

Figure B-2: *The Netscape aquarium at 20:04:11 GMT on October 25, 1995.*

GLOSSARY

alias   A nickname used, for example, in e-mail managers so that you can enter "fred" and your e-mail manager knows you mean "edf556@froward.cursci.com."

anchor   In hypertext, the object that is highlighted and "clickable." It may be a word, a phrase, or an inline image.

anonymous FTP   An FTP service that serves any user, not just users having accounts at the site. Anonymous FTP generally permits downloading of all files, but uploading only into a directory called "/incoming."

Archie   A keyword search service that searches the directory and file titles of all FTP sites that are indexed.

ASCII (American Standard Code for Information Interchange)   An agreed-upon coding of letters, numbers, and symbols. An ASCII file is one that makes use of only the first 128 ASCII symbols—the symbols you see on your keyboard, basically. The advantage of ASCII files is that one bit per byte is always available for purposes such as error-checking.

.AU   In hypermedia, an audio file format common in DOS systems.

.AVI   A combined video/audio compressed file format developed by Microsoft.

backbone   The connections between the primary computers in a network. Stub networks branch off the backbone.

bandwidth   Used (somewhat inaccurately) to express the maximum possible throughput of a data link in bits per second. A so-called T1 line has a bandwidth of 1.544 Mbps.

beta (release) software   Software that is not considered finished enough to market, but is released so that the general public (or a selected population) can participate in the development process by trying it out and reporting bugs. So called because *alpha* debugging is done before any public release. Netscape Communications Corporation has a general policy of releasing several betas before each commercial version—often these are designed to "self-destruct" after a period of time judged adequate for all bugs to be discovered.

binary   A numbering system used in computing, which has two as its base. A binary file, as opposed to an ASCII file, makes use of 256 symbols and so does not keep a bit free for error-checking.

bookmark   A Web address in the form of a URL that a user keeps an easily obtainable record of in order to be able to return to it quickly.

cache   1. An area of RAM set aside to hold data or instructions that would normally be read from disk, in order to speed up access to it. 2. In network operation, an area of disk set aside to hold data that would normally be read from the Net, for the same reason. Netscape Navigator makes use of both types of cache.

CD-ROM   A compact disk formatted to act as data storage for a PC. The "ROM" part (Read Only Memory) is a reminder that, just like a music CD, you can read information from it but you can't write new information to it.

check box   A very small active area of a Windows dialog box that has only two states, checked and unchecked. You can toggle between the two states with mouse clicks.

client/server software   An arrangement of computers, very common in Internet systems, whereby a small system called the client makes use of the data management services of a much larger computer, the server. Netscape Navigator is a client/server system, with the client running on your machine taking advantage of the far greater processing power of the server at a remote site.

clipboard   In Windows applications, a part of computer memory used as temporary storage for any text, picture, or object that the user places there using "Edit/Copy" or "Edit/Cut" (or keyboard equivalents). The object remains on the clipboard until replaced or until the end of the Windows session. The purpose is to enable the object to be reinserted using "Edit/Paste" or Ctrl-V into a different position or to a completely different Windows application. The contents of the clipboard can be seen at any time using the Windows Clipboard Viewer.

Content window   The portion of the Netscape Navigator screen in which actual page content is seen, as opposed to the control and information portions.

cropping   Cutting off unwanted borders from a photograph or other graphic image to correct framing errors or to bring out a detail. In computer graphics, it's done with a "crop-box" drawn across the artwork with the mouse.

cyberspace   Fanciful term coined by William Gibson in the novel *Neuromancer* to describe the sum total of computer-accessible information in the world.

dial-up account   The type of Internet access account that is connected only when a modem connection is established, as distinct from a direct permanent connection. Often used to refer to a shell account as opposed to a SLIP- or PPP-type access, even though SLIP/PPP accounts frequently are also established by dial-up.

direct connection   A hard-wired connection between a computer and the Internet, giving the computer an IP address and the ability to function as a Web site.

directory   A logical division of a computer data storage device, such as a disk drive, in which files are grouped in a way that makes sense to the user. All Jane's memos in the C:\JANE\MEMOS directory, is a simple example. See also **folder**.

DNS (Domain Name Server)   Software that converts host names to IP addresses.

drag and drop   A mouse operation that allows the user to click on a screen icon and, by holding down the mouse button, move it (or a "shadow" of it) to another part of the screen. When the mouse button is released, some appropriate event happens, such as copying a file to a new location or application.

.EXE file extension   In DOS, denotes an "executable" file that will run if its name is simply entered at the DOS prompt (with or without the .EXE). Files that are executable in Windows also frequently have the extension .EXE.

external image An image that may be accessed by a hypertext link from an HTML page, but is not automatically displayed when the page loads, as is an **inline image**.

FAQ (Frequently Asked Questions) Pronounced "FAK." Shorthand for an information file about some system. In Usenet newsgroups, you should always read any FAQs you can find because if you ask a question that's already covered in the FAQ you are likely to be "flamed" (see **flame**).

Finger Originally a UNIX command requesting information about another registered UNIX account holder. Now available to Netscape Navigator by courtesy of Finger "gateways."

flame A deliberately abusive message in e-mail or Usenet postings.

folder A logical grouping of files in disk storage. The term was familiar to Macintosh users, but not to DOS/Windows users, until Windows 95. Win95 uses the "folder" convention extensively in its file structure displays, to indicate a group of files having something in common, but the older DOS "directory" structure still exists.

FTP (File Transfer Protocol) One of the original protocols on the Internet, which allows for very efficient transfer of entire data files between computers but discourages interactive browsing.

.GIF (Graphics Interchange Format) One of many formats for computerized images, designed to be highly transportable between computer systems. Ideal for line art, and very frequently used for inline images in Web pages.

Gopher   An Internet search-and-display application that reduces all Internet resource "trees" to onscreen menus.

grayed   Most Windows applications, Netscape Navigator included, have an extensive choice of toolbar buttons and menu options. However, not all of these options may be actually available at any given moment. (For example, the Paste option is not available when nothing is on the clipboard.) Rather than eliminate these options altogether, software designers arrange to display them in a pale color rather than in a sharp and contrasted fashion. They are then said to be "grayed out."

helper applications   Applications that cooperate with Netscape Navigator and other Web browsers to perform functions that Navigator itself is not programmed to perform, such as viewing video files.

hexadecimal   An arithmetical system, used in computer programming, that has 16 as the base instead of 10. The first sixteen numbers in hex are 1,2,3,4,5,6,7,8,9,A,B,C,D,E,F,10.

home page   1. Whatever page you designate (in the General/Appearance preference panel) as the Web page you want Netscape Navigator to load at startup. 2. A personal page you control and refer other people to.

host   A computer whose primary function is facilitating communications.

hotlist   A personal list of favorite Web addresses, organized so that it creates hypertext links to the addresses. Same as a **bookmark** list.

HTML (HyperText Markup Language) A convention for inserting "tags" into a text file that Web browsers like Netscape Navigator can interpret to display or link to hypermedia. HTML files usually have the extension .HTML or .HTM.

hypermedia Media such as video and audio, which go beyond what was thought (not so very long ago!) to be the realm of personal computer display.

hypertext A system of interactive text linking that allows the reader to choose any path through the sum total of available text.

icon On a Windows desktop, a small image representing a dormant application or program group that can be brought to life by double-clicking. In a Web page, a small image that may or may not be a hyperlink to some other resource.

inline image On a Web page, an image to be loaded along with the page text (although inline images can be suppressed by a Netscape Navigator user to speed up page loading).

Internet A network of computer networks stretching across the world, linking computers of many different types. No one organization has control of the Internet or jurisdiction over it.

IP address An Internet machine address formatted with numbers rather than a host name. An IP address may also contain a port number, separated from the host address by a colon.

ISP Internet Service Provider.

Java   A system invented by Sun Microsystems, now embedded in Netscape Navigator, enabling dynamic objects called "applets" to be transmitted through HTTP server-client links. Animated pictures are an example. **Hot Java** is separate client software designed specifically to display Java applets.

.JPEG (Joint Photographic Experts Group)   A modern image file format allowing for a choice of three levels of file compression, with progressive trade-off of image quality. JPEGs are ideal for photographic art, as opposed to line art which compresses better in .GIF format.

LAN (Local Area Network)   A group of computers and peripherals that are interlinked to share resources in a restricted area, typically an office building. Although Netscape Navigator was designed for the World Wide Web, its nifty hyperlink features make it very suitable for operation within a LAN .

link   In the World Wide Web context, short for "hypertext link," meaning a path a user may follow that connects one part of a document to another part of the same document, a different document, or some other resource.

Lynx   The name of a text-only World Wide Web browser, available for UNIX, Linux, DOS, and a few other operating systems.

mail server   A computer whose primary function is e-mail management for a group of subscribers.

MIME (Multipurpose Internet Mail Extensions)   A set of agreed-upon formats enabling binary files to be sent as e-mail or attached to e-mail. "MIME types" have come to mean hypermedia formats in general, even when not communicated by e-mail.

mirror site   A subsidiary FTP site that has the same content as the main site that it reflects. Used to take the load off sites that are so popular that they are frequently inaccessible because of congestion.

Mosaic   A World Wide Web graphical browser; the forerunner of Netscape Navigator.

Mozilla   Pet name the software authors gave to Netscape Navigator during development, which has survived as the name of the green monster who decorates many of the Netscape information pages and as the "Mozilla DTD," the HTML version that includes the Netscape extensions.

.MPEG (Motion Picture Experts Group)   Modern standard format for compression and storage of video hypermedia files.

NCSA (National Center for Supercomputing Applications)   A U.S. Government center at the University of Illinois. NCSA developed the Mosaic Web browser and other Internet interfaces.

NEWSRC file   A data file that keeps a record of which newsgroups a user is subscribed to, and which articles have already been read.

newsreader   Software whose function is to interact with Usenet newsgroups, providing services such as subscription, display, follow-up, print, download, and so on.

NNTP (Network News Transport Protocol)   The protocol used by the Usenet newsgroups to disseminate bulletins.

packet-switching   A system, used extensively throughout the Internet, for handling messages based upon the breakdown of a message into standardized packets, each of which is independently routed to the addressee.

pane   A sub-section of a Window. For example, the Netscape Navigator mail window has three panes: the folder pane, the mail pane, and the message pane. The boundaries between panes can be moved by the user.

path   A complete instruction defining where in a computer's directory structure a certain file is located. A path may be indicated from the root, such as "C:\WINDOWS\WINAPPS\GAMES, or relative to the current sub-directory. "..\WINAPPS\ACCOUNTS" means "starting from here, go up one level then back down to WINAPPS\ACCOUNTS."

POP mail (Post Office Protocol)   An e-mail system that establishes your primary mailbox in your own desktop computer rather than at your access provider's site. POP mail is the usual protocol for incoming mail, while SMTP is used for outgoing.

PPP (Point-to-Point Protocol)   A convention for transmitting packet-switched data.

Properties window   The pull-down window displaying hidden information about some object selected with the mouse. Properties windows usually, but not always, allow the user to edit the information.

proxy   A device used to access the Internet around a "firewall" put up to ensure security against unauthorized access in a large system.

QuickTime   A video format originally invented for Macintosh multimedia systems but now also available for DOS/Windows; also the software that allows you to play QuickTime movies.

RAM (Random Access Memory)   The part of a computer's memory that is available for loading user-selected software and data.

ROM (Read Only Memory)   The part of a computer's memory that contains manufacturer's instructions; it is not available for the user.

search engine   A keyword searching algorithm or complete software package including search algorithms.

server   The server half of a client/server pair: the computer that handles the primary data management tasks on behalf of its clients.

SGML (Standard Generalized Markup Language)   The forerunner of HTML; it is still used for many documents on the Web, particularly reference works. Embedded "tags" similar to HTML tags describe the format of the document so that it can be displayed "across platforms," meaning on any computer system.

shell   A simple, usually menu-driven, interface that shields a computer user from the complexities of operating systems such as UNIX. Hence a common type of Internet connection, known as a "UNIX shell account," can be operated efficiently with extremely limited actual knowledge of UNIX.

.SIG or **signature file**   A short text file that you habitually use as your personal sign-off at the end of e-mail and/or Usenet postings. Netscape Navigator and other Internet applications make it possible for your .SIG to be appended to outgoing messages automatically.

SLIP (Serial Line Internet Protocol)   A convention for transmitting packet-switched data.

SMTP (Simple Mail Transfer Protocol)   The usual protocol for outgoing Internet e-mail.

socket   One of a series of memory addresses in a computer reserved for data exchange with a TCP/IP stack.

source document   In the World Wide Web, the raw file that an HTML author creates, as distinct from a Web page which is the representation of a source document in hypertext.

stack   In the context of TCP/IP, the ordered series of protocols and packet drivers required to interface a desktop computer with the Internet.

string   In computerese, any sequence of characters. "Desktop/412" is a string. So is "µ668_counter‰." Basically, any variable used by a computer that cannot necessarily be evaluated numerically is called a string.

tag   The name given to the code strings embedded in HTML documents, such as <H1>, which means a level 1 heading.

TCP/IP (Transmission Control Protocol/Internet Protocol)   Shorthand for the most common packet-switching protocols used on the Internet.

Telnet   A software system that establishes a connection between two computers for the purpose of data exchange. Unlike FTP, Telnet is interactive and, as commonly used, makes a desktop computer behave as though it were the workstation of a much larger computer.

.TIFF (Tagged Image File Format)   A standard format for storing hypermedia image files. A .TIFF file is uncompressed (and therefore generally large) and can contain many images.

toolbar   The area of a computer application screen used in conjunction with a mouse pointer to perform various functions by clicking. The active areas of a toolbar are usually drawn to look like push buttons, and often have different "in" and "out" renderings.

Trumpet Winsock   A popular Winsock package (TCP/IP stack) designed by Peter Tattam of the University of Tasmania. (See also **Winsock**.)

UNIX   The operating system of choice for computers dedicated to the Internet. UNIX is inherently suited to network operations.

URL (Universal Resource Locator)   An address that completely defines a resource of the World Wide Web. A URL has four elements:

- The service—http or ftp or a few others.
- The host—the computer that handles the resource.
- The port number (often not necessary because it defaults according to the service requested).
- The path and filename of the resource.

The format of a URL is: service://host:port/path.

Usenet   A worldwide network exchanging "articles" or messages posted by individual contributors grouped under subject categories called "newsgroups." Most newsgroups are open, and anyone may contribute. Netscape Navigator has its own built-in newsreader for interacting with Usenet. (See also **newsreader**.)

Veronica   An online keyword searcher for the Gopher.

WAIS (Wide Area Information Service)   A database service of the Internet allowing structured searching for keyword combinations. WAIS supplies a measure of how well documents it finds match your keywords in the form of a "relevance score," with a score of 1000 being a perfect match.

.WAV   A standard format for storing hypermedia audio files.

Web   Short for the World Wide Web.

Web browser   A user interface to the Web. Netscape Navigator is a graphical Web browser.

Web crawler   Software that searches the Web (or more commonly, a database *derived* from the Web) for keywords input by a user.

Web page   A coherent document that is readable by a Web browser. A Web page may vary in complexity all the way from a simple piece of text enclosed by the HTML tags <PRE>...</PRE>, meaning "pre-formatted," to a densely coded HTML file giving the user access to many types of hypermedia.

Web server   A server computer equipped to offer World Wide Web access to its clients.

Web spider   A type of keyword search software.

Webmaster   A person at a Web server site who is qualified to administer all Web resources at that site.

Winsock   Short for Windows Sockets. The interface between your Windows version of Netscape Navigator and the TCP/IP stack you are running.

World Wide Web   The arrangement of Internet-accessible resources, including hypertext and hypermedia, addressed by URLs.

zine   Any online magazine.

INDEX

M

N

O

Open toolbar button 38, 42
Options menu bar item 51–52

P

<P> tag 142
Page Setup menu option 44
PaintShopPro 119–120
Panels
   Helper 116
   Mail and News Composition 107
Panorama 129
Paper Software 127
Paris Pages internet site 183
PC Magazine internet site 172
PC Week internet site 172
Pdf (Portable Document Format) files 128
Point-to-Point Protocol (PPP) 14
POP (Post Office Protocol) 66
Portable Document Format (pdf) files 128
Post and reply button 87
Post Office Protocol (POP) 66
Post reply button 87
Posting to newsgroups 87–88
PPP (Point-to-Point Protocol) 14
Preferences
   Appearance panel 101
   apps 103
   colors 102–103
   fonts 102
   helper applications 26, 104–106
   identity 25
   link styles 101
   Mail and News 106–110
   Network 110–111
   saving 52
   Security 111–112
   servers 25
Print menu option 39, 45
Print Preview menu option 45
Print toolbar button 39, 45

Printing
   3D horizontal rules 44
   inline images 39, 44
   preview 39, 45
   setup 44
   web documents 39
Private Eye internet site 172
Prizewinning internet sites 186
Progress bar 62–63
Progressive JPEG images 118

Q

QuickTime video format 121
QVTNET helper application 134

R

RealAudio audio player 126
Real-time audio internet sites 126
Real-time video 126–127
Reference internet sites 183–185
Refresh menu option 47
Registration Information menu option 57
Release Notes menu option 58
Reload Frame menu option 47
Reload menu option 37, 47
Reload toolbar button 37
Reload web page 37
Reply button 87
Reply-to address 109
Resizing inline images 120
Restaurant le Cordon Bleu internet site 174
Right mouse button menu
   Back option 35
   Forward option 35
   image menu 59
   link menu 59
   mail menu 75
   Newsnet menu 89
ROT13 73–74, 88

S

T

X

 # Y

 # Z

Internet Resources

The Windows Internet Tour Guide, Second Edition

$29.95, 424 pages, illustrated, Part #: 174-0

This runaway bestseller has been updated to include Ventana Mosaic™, the hot Web reader, along with graphical software for e-mail, file downloading, news-reading and more. Noted for its down-to-earth documentation, the new edition features expanded listings and a look at Net developments. Includes three companion disks.

Walking the World Wide Web, Second Edition

$39.95, 500 pages, illustrated, Part #: 298-4

A listing that never goes out of date! This groundbreaking bestseller includes a CD-ROM enhanced with Ventana's WebWalker™ technology, and updated online components that make it the richest resource available for Web travelers.

HTML Publishing With Internet Assistant

$29.95, 280 pages, illustrated, Part #: 273-9

Microsoft's Internet Assistant makes translating Word documents into Web documents as easy as saving a file! Learn how this free add-on lets you easily create effective Internet documents without knowing a line of code.

HTML Publishing on the Internet for Windows
HTML Publishing on the Internet for Macintosh

$49.95, 512 pages, illustrated, Windows Part #: 229-1, Macintosh Part #: 228-3

Successful publishing for the Internet requires an understanding of "nonlinear" presentation as well as specialized software. Both are here. Learn how HTML builds the hot links that let readers choose their own paths—and how to use effective design to drive your message for them. The enclosed CD-ROM includes Netscape Navigator, HoTMetaL LITE, graphic viewer, templates conversion software and more!

Acrobat Quick Tour

$14.95, 280 pages, illustrated, Part #: 255-0

In the three-ring circus of electronic publishing, Adobe® Acrobat® is turning cartwheels around the competition. Learn the key tools and features of Acrobat's base components in this hands-on guide that includes a look at the emerging world of document exchange.

Internet Guide for Windows 95

$24.95, 552 pages, illustrated, Part #: 260-7

The *Internet Guide for Windows 95* shows how to use Windows 95's built-in communications tools to access and navigate the Net. Whether you're using The Microsoft Network or an independent Internet provider and Microsoft *Plus!*, this easy-to-read guide helps you started quickly and easily. Learn how to e-mail, download files, and navigate the World Wide Web and take a tour of top sites. An *Online Companion* on Ventana Online features hypertext links to top sites listed in the book.

Books marked with this logo include a free Internet *Online Companion*™, featuring archives of free utilities plus a software archive and links to other Internet resources.

Insightful Guides

Looking Good in Print, Third Edition

$24.95, 462 pages, illustrated in full color, Part #: 047-7

For use with any software or hardware, this desktop design bible has become the standard among novice and experienced desktop publishers alike. With more than 300,000 copies in print, *Looking Good in Print, Third Edition* is even better—with new sections on photography and scanning. Learn the fundamentals of professional-quality design along with tips on resources and reference materials.

Looking Good in Color

$29.95, 272 pages, illustrated in full color, Part # 219-4

Like effective design, using color properly is an essential part of a desktop publishing investment. This richly illustrated four-color book addresses basic issues from color theory—through computer technologies, printing processes and budget issues—to final design. Even the graphically challenged can make immediate use of the practical advice in *Looking Good in Color*.

Microsoft Office 95 Companion 🌐

$34.95, 1144 pages, illustrated, Part #: 188-0

This all-in-one reference to Microsoft's red-hot suite is a worthy sequel to Ventana's bestselling *Windows, Word & Excel Office Companion*. Covers basic commands and features, as well as dozens of tips and tricks not found in the program manuals. Includes a section on using Windows 95. The companion disk contains samples, exercises, software and sample files from the book.

Voodoo Mac, 2nd Edition
Voodoo Windows 95

$24.95, 504 pages, illustrated, Macintosh Part #: 177-5, Windows Part #: 145-7

Whether you're a power user looking for new shortcuts or a beginner trying to make sense of it all, *Voodoo* books have something for everyone! Computer veteran Kay Nelson has compiled hundreds of invaluable tips, tricks, hints and shortcuts that simplify your computing tasks and save time, including disk and drive magic, font and printing tips, alias alchemy and more! Companion disk includes free utilities, graphics and shortcuts.

The Windows 95 Book

$39.95, 1232 pages, illustrated, Part #: 154-6

The anxiously awaited revamp of Windows is finally here—which means new working styles for PC users. This new handbook offers an insider's look at the all-new interface—arming users with tips and techniques for file management, desktop design, optimizing and much more. A must-have for moving to *95!* The companion CD-ROM features tutorials, demos, previews and online help plus utilities, screen savers, wallpaper and sounds.

The System 7.5 Book, Third Edition

$24.95, 736 pages, illustrated, Part #: 129-5

The all-time best-selling *System 7 Book*, now revised, updated and retitled! *The System 7.5 Book* is the industry's recognized standard and the last word on the Macintosh and PowerMac operating systems. A complete overview of AppleHelp, AOCE, e-mail, fax, PC Exchange, MacTCP, QuickTime and more!

Check your local bookstore or software retailer for these and other bestselling titles, or call toll free:

800/743-5369

Now book the extended excursion.

Sure, you've taken the Quick Tour.

But this time, slow down, unpack and explore. Poke around the side streets and back alleys of Netscape Navigator 2.0's enhanced navigation tools. Learn how others are doing business on the Net. Discover how becoming "Netscape fluent" can help you increase your productivity—not to mention your pleasure—as you travel the Internet.

The *Official Netscape Navigator 2.0 Book.* More than 500 pages of tips, techniques, illustrations and examples. Get to know how the natives live. The companion CD-ROM contains a free, fully supported copy of Netscape Navigator 2.0, the latest commercial version of the Web's leading, full-featured browser.

US: $29.95 • CAD: $41.95
Windows edition: part # 347-6
Macintosh edition: part # 413-8

To order any Ventana title, complete this order form and mail or fax it to us, with payment, for quick shipment.

TITLE	PART #	QUANTITY	PRICE	TOTAL

SHIPPING:

For all standard orders, please ADD $4.50/first book, $1.35/each additional.
For "two-day air," ADD $8.25/first book/ $2.25/each additional.
For orders to Canada, ADD $6.50/book.
For orders sent C.O.D., ADD $4.50 to your shipping rate.
North Carolina Residents must ADD 6% sales tax.
International orders require additional shipping charges.

SUBTOTAL = $ _____
SHIPPING = $ _____
TOTAL = $ _____

Name _____ Daytime telephone _____

Company _____

Address (No PO Box) _____

City _____ State _____ Zip _____

____ Payment enclosed ____ VISA ____ MC Acc't # _____ Exp. date _____

Signature _____ Exact name on card _____

Mail to: Ventana • PO Box 13964 • Research Triangle Park, NC 27709-3964 ☎ 800/743-5369 • Fax 919/544-9472

Check your local bookstore or software retailer for these and other bestselling titles, or call toll free **800/743-5369.**